BUILDING EFFECTIVE TEAMS

DUKE CORPORATE EDUCATION

LEADING FROM THE CENTER

BUILDING EFFECTIVE TEAMS

Dearborn™
Trade Publishing
A Kaplan Professional Company

President, Dearborn Publishing: Roy Lipner
Vice President and Publisher: Cynthia A. Zigmund
Acquisitions Editor: Jon Malysiak
Senior Project Editor: Trey Thoelcke
Interior Design: Lucy Jenkins
Cover Design: Design Solutions
Typesetting: Elizabeth Pitts

Published by Dearborn Trade Publishing
A Kaplan Professional Company

Printed in the United States of America

05 06 07 10 9 8 7 6 5 4 3 2 1

Library of Congress Cataloging-in-Publication Data

Building effective teams / Duke Corporate Education.
p. cm. – (Leading from the center)
Includes bibliographical references and index.
ISBN 0-7931-9523-3
1. Teams in the workplace–Management. I. Duke Corporate Education. II. Series.
HD66.B834 2005
658.4′022–dc22

2005010658

CONTENTS

Acknowledgments vii

Introduction ix

1. THE CHALLENGE OF BUILDING AND LEADING EFFECTIVE TEAMS 1

2. WHAT RESULTS DO YOU NEED? 13

3. DO YOU HAVE WHAT YOU NEED? 25

4. HOW WILL YOU WORK AS A TEAM? 41

5. HOW WILL YOU WORK ACROSS BOUNDARIES? 57

6. TAKING THE PULSE AND MANAGING DYNAMICALLY 71

7. GROWING TRENDS 79

Bibliography 87

Index 89

ACKNOWLEDGMENTS

First and foremost, we want to thank our clients and the many program participants around the globe. We begin our work by listening to our clients and gaining an understanding of their business challenges. Working with talented clients and actively engaging in their challenges across a range of industries and geographies has afforded us the opportunity to learn and develop an informed point of view on these topics. We thank them for trusting in our approach and making us part of their team.

We also are fortunate to have an extensive network of faculty, coaches, facilitators, and partners who believe in our mission and have agreed to join in our adventure. Together we have delivered programs in 37 different countries since Duke Corporate Education (Duke CE) was formed in July 2000. We absolutely could not have accomplished what we have and learned what we know without them.

John Tolsma, along with his colleagues at erroyo, has been a close partner for several years. As John worked with us, he came to believe that we have something unique to say and urged us to capture our ideas in these books. He introduced us to our editors at Dearborn Trade, and the rest, as they say, is history. Jon Malysiak and Trey Thoelcke continue to patiently guide us through this process. We can't thank them enough.

As with any organization, we too have created a shorthand that accelerates our own conversation, though it doesn't translate well outside Duke CE. We were lucky to have the writing and editing assistance of Elizabeth Brack, who worked with us over the many versions and edits of these chapters to make the words flow more smoothly.

Throughout the book you will find several graphical images reinforcing the surrounding ideas. Ryan Stevens worked with us to capture our thoughts and ideas and turn them into the Figures included within these pages; often working with vague instructions, such as "It should feel like 'this.'" He did a wonderful job.

We especially thank our extremely talented and busy panel of experts who graciously agreed to offer their thoughts on the Managing Day-to-Day scenarios. Bob Fulmer, Tom Colligan, Bob Reinheimer, and Michael Serino combine for many years of experience and offer great insights to the multifaceted problems facing the managers in our examples.

Without a doubt the busiest person at Duke CE, our CEO, Blair Sheppard, was instrumental to this effort. He supported the initiative from the outset and, more importantly, always made time to review our output and guide our thinking. His assistance is without measure. We could not have done it without him.

At one point during the many weeks we spent working on this book—engaging clients, researching, talking, writing, editing, and then cycling back to the beginning—we came across a statement that this book will hopefully disprove. It essentially said that no great works (musical compositions, novels, and the like) can be created by a team—the thought being that they require the guiding vision and creativity of a single, uniquely talented individual. Although our book certainly isn't in the category of "great literary works," we take immense pride that this, like our client work, has been indeed very much a team effort.

We've drawn upon the insights, experiences, and expertise from numerous colleagues here at Duke CE. We hope that the content of this book stimulates your thinking and improves your ability to act and to solve the strategic challenges confronting you.

The *Building Effective Teams* writing team: Michael Canning, Marla Tuchinsky, and Cindy Campbell.

INTRODUCTION

In the past 30 years, they have been repeatedly laid off, outsourced, replaced by information technology applications, and insulted with such derogatory names as "the cement layer." Their bosses accused them of distorting and disrupting communication in their organizations, and their subordinates accused them of thwarting the subordinates' autonomy and empowerment. Who are "they"? Middle managers, those managing in the middle of the organization.

With such treatment, you might think that middle managers are villainous evildoers who sabotage companies, or obstructionist bureaucrats who stand in the way of real work getting done. However, the reality is just the opposite. When performed well, the middle manager role is critical in organizations.

Although over the past several decades the value and stature of middle managers has seen both high and low points, we at Duke Corporate Education believe that managing in the center of the organization has always been both critically important and personally demanding. As one would expect, the essence of the role—the required mind-set and skill set—has continued to change over time. The need to update each of these dimensions is driven by periodic shifts in such underlying forces as marketplace dynamics, technology, organizational structure, and employee expectations. Now and then, these forces converge to create a point of inflection that calls for a "step change" in how organizations are governed, with particular implications for those managing in the center.

In the *Leading from the Center* series, we examine some of these primary causes that are shaping what it means to successfully lead from the center in the modern organization. We outline the emerging imperative for middle management in an organization as well as the mind-set, knowledge, and skills required to successfully navigate through the most prevalent challenges that lie ahead.

THE NEW CENTER

There are four powerful and pervasive trends affecting the role that managers in the center of an organization are being asked to assume. These trends–information technology, industry convergence, globalization, and regulations–connect directly to the challenges these managers are facing.

Compared to twenty or thirty years ago, *information technology* has escalated the amount, speed, and availability of data to the point that it has changed the way we work and live. Access to information has shifted more power to our customers and suppliers. They not only have more information, but are directly involved in and interacting with the various processes along the value chain. On a personal level, we now find ourselves connected to other people all the time; cell phones, pagers, BlackBerrys, and PDAs all reinforce the 24/7 culture. The transition from work week to weekend and back is less distinct. These micro-transitions happen all day, every day because many of us remain connected all the time.

Industries previously seen as separate are now seeing multiple points of *convergence.* Think about how digital technology has led to a convergence of sound, image, text, computing, and communications. Longstanding industry boundaries and parameters are gone (e.g., cable television companies are in the phone business, electronics companies sell music), and along with them, the basis and nature of competition. The boundaries are blurred. It's clear that new possibilities, opportunities, and directions exist, but it isn't always clear what managers should do. Managers will have to be prepared to adapt; their role is to observe, learn from experience, and set direction dynamically. Layered on top of this is the need to manage a more complex set of relationships–cooperating on Monday, competing on Tuesday, and partnering on Wednesday.

Globalization means that assets are now distributed and configured around the world to serve customers and gain competitive advantage. Even companies that consider themselves local interact with global organizations. There is more reliance on fast-developing regional centers of expertise. For example, computer programming in India and manufacturing in China. This means that middle managers are interacting with and coordinating the efforts of people who live in different cultures, and may be awake while their managers are asleep. The notion of a workday has changed as the work straddles time zones. The nature of leading has changed as it becomes more common to partner with vendors and work in virtual teams across regions.

The first three forces are causing shifts in the fourth—the *regulatory environment.* Many industries are experiencing more regulation, while a few others are experiencing less. In some arenas now experiencing more regulation, there is also a drive for more accountability. Demand for more accountability leads to a greater desire to clarify boundaries and roles. Yet there is more ambiguity as to what the rules are and how best to operationalize them. Consider how, in the wake of Sarbanes-Oxley legislation, U.S. companies and their accountants continue to sort through the new requirements, while rail companies in Britain are negotiating which company is responsible for maintaining what stretch of tracks. Middle managers sit where regulations get implemented and are a critical force in shaping how companies respond to the shifts in the environment.

All of these changes have implications for those managing at the center of organizations. No small group at the top can have the entire picture because the environment has more of everything: more information and connectivity, a faster pace, a dynamic competitive space, greater geographic reach, better informed and connected customers and suppliers, and shifting legal rules of the game. No small group can process the implications, make thoughtful decisions and disseminate clear action steps. The top of the organization needs those in the center to help make sense of the dynamic environment. The connection between strategy development and strategy execution becomes less linear and more interdependent and, therefore, managers in the center become pivotal actors.

As we said earlier, the notion of the middle of an organization typically conjures up a vertical image depicting managers in the center of a hierarchy. This mental image carries with it a perception of those managers as gatekeepers—controlling the pace at which information or resources flow down or up. It appears to be simple and linear.

However, as many of you are no doubt experiencing, you now find yourselves navigating in a matrix, and as a node in a network or

FIGURE I.1 In the Center of the Action

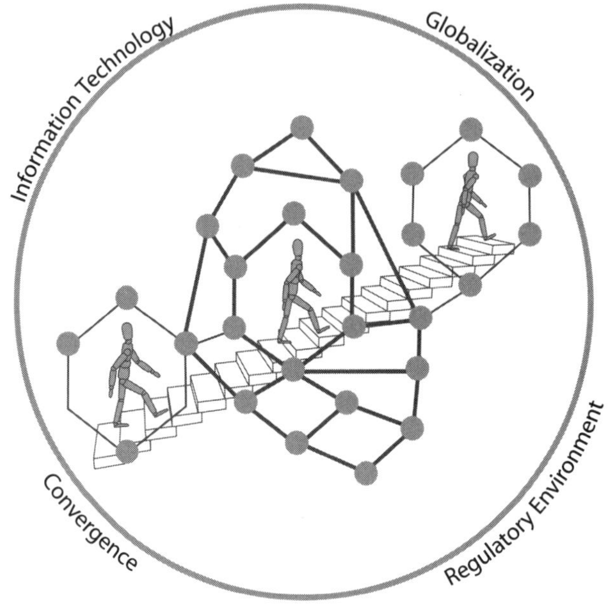

multiple networks. As depicted in Figure I.1, this new view of the center conjures up images of centrality, integration, connection, and catalyst. *You are in the center of the action, not the middle of a hierarchy.* When you overlay this connected view on the traditional vertical notion, it produces some interesting tensions, trade offs, and opportunities. Your formal authority runs vertically, but your real power to achieve results stems from your ability to work across all levels and boundaries.

IF YOU ARE LEADING FROM THE CENTER

If you are a manager in the center today, you have many hats to wear, more balls to juggle, and fewer certainties in your work environment. You have to be adaptive yet provide continuity in your leadership. You need to simultaneously translate strategy, influence and collaborate, lead teams, coach and motivate, support innovation, and own the systems and processes—all in the service of getting results. Those in the center need more courage than ever. You are the conscience of your organization, carrying forth the values, and at the same time you build today's and tomorrow's business success.

Strategy Translator

As a strategy translator, you must first understand the corporate strategy and determine what parts of it your group can best support. Next, you must translate it into an action plan for your group, making sure it aligns well to the overall strategy. You'll need to consider which projects are essential stepping stones and which are needed in their own right, and establish some priorities or guiding goals. You must then communicate the details of the plan and priorities, and create momentum around them. As your team implements, you'll need to involve not only your people but to also collaborate and coordinate with others, including peers, customers, and other units. Instead of directing a one way downward flow of information, you must translate upward as well and act as a conduit for strategic feedback to the executives above.

Influencer and Collaborator for Results

Middle managers must learn how to make things happen by influencing, integrating, and collaborating across the boundaries of the organization. As a manager, instead of focusing exclusively on your piece, you have to look outside of your own group to develop a network of supporting relationships. Rather than issuing commands and asserting power based on your position, you have to use other tactics to gain agreement and make things happen.

Leader of Teams

Teams have become a one-size-fits-all solution for organizing work in today's economy—virtual teams, project teams, product teams, and function-specific teams—and can be either the blessing or the bane of many companies. Your role as a manager includes understanding the challenges of teams and facilitating their development so that they can be effective more quickly. You have to align the team's energy and talents in a way that will deliver the desired results. You are responsible for creating an environment that will help this group of people work well together to achieve today's objectives and to develop the skills needed to take on future goals.

Coach and Motivator

Many organizations are well positioned to execute their strategies in yesterday's environment, they are moderately able to meet their current needs, and often they are not thinking about how to position themselves for the future. From the center of the organization, middle managers assume much of the responsibility for their people. They create an environment to attract and retain good employees, coach them to do their current jobs better, and bear primary responsibility for developing others. As a manager, you must figure out how to build the next level of capability, protect existing people, connect their aspirations to opportunities for development, and make work more enjoyable. You need to provide regular feedback—both positive and redirecting—and build strong relationships with those who surround you. If done well, your departments will be more efficient and your employees will be better equipped to become leaders in their own right.

Intrapreneur/Innovator

Enabling and supporting an innovative approach within your company will foster the strategic direction of the future. To effectively sponsor innovation, you need to create the context for your people, foster a climate that supports innovative efforts, and actively sponsor the ideas of the future. You have to *be* innovative and *lead* the innovative efforts of others. Innovation is most often associated with new-product development, but innovative approaches also are needed in developing new services or solving internal system and process problems. As a manager, you use your influence and relationships to find the root cause of problems, and the resources to make change happen.

Owner of Systems and Processes

You need to understand that part of your role is to take ownership for architecting new systems and processes. You will have to shift your thinking from living within existing systems and processes to making sure that those systems and processes work well: Do the systems and processes support or get in the way of progress? One of the mistakes we have made in the past is to not hold managers accountable for their role in architecting the next generation of systems and processes. As a manager, you must perform harsh audits of existing systems, and understand when to tear down what may have been left in place from a past strategy. You need to assess what is no longer relevant and/or is no longer working. Part of your responsibility is to think about and decide whether to re-engineer or remove existing systems.

SHIFTS IN MIND-SET NEEDED FOR THE FUTURE

What impact are these trends and this new center of the organization having on teams as we know them? What do all of these changes mean for the manager who is responsible for helping these teams quickly form and operate effectively? The "typical" team of the past–five or six people who work exclusively with each other and sit near each other in a central office–is no longer the norm in many organizations. Building and leading teams today requires a new mind-set in how we define them, how we manage them, and how we help them to quickly become effective.

Many of the basic tenets that have traditionally been touted as critical for working effectively as a team are still valid and shouldn't be completely discarded. It's still important to align with a clear purpose and to manage the dynamics within the team, but things are changing. These basic elements of working in teams are now overlaid by the speed at which teams have to form and produce results, the distance from which they communicate and work together, and the fluctuating boundaries of team membership.

In this book, we'll discuss the traditional elements of building effective teams that are still useful, and we'll provide some tips for successfully navigating and managing the new complexities of today's teams.

CHAPTER ONE

1

THE CHALLENGE OF BUILDING AND LEADING EFFECTIVE TEAMS

IN THIS CHAPTER

The Value of Teams ■ What Is a Team? ■ The Manager's Role ■ Today's Special Challenges

THE VALUE OF TEAMS

People have always worked in collaborative units–either for the camaraderie and social interactions with others, or for the benefits of their diverse points of view, support, and skills. There have always been tasks too great for one person to tackle alone, such as early tribes hunting large animals, or tasks that require people with different skills and talents to complete, such as playing a Mozart symphony, building a space capsule, or constructing a modern house. Teams are a fundamental unit of organizing people to meet new challenges and achieve results.

While the context, types of challenges, and people's knowledge, skills, and expectations have shifted dramatically over the years, the fundamental need for teams has not gone away. As the quality of tools and technology continues to advance, so does the complexity of the challenges we undertake. More and more, the problems we face are so complex that they require multiple perspectives and different types of expertise to solve. In addition, the time to capture

FIGURE 1.1 Factors Affecting Teams

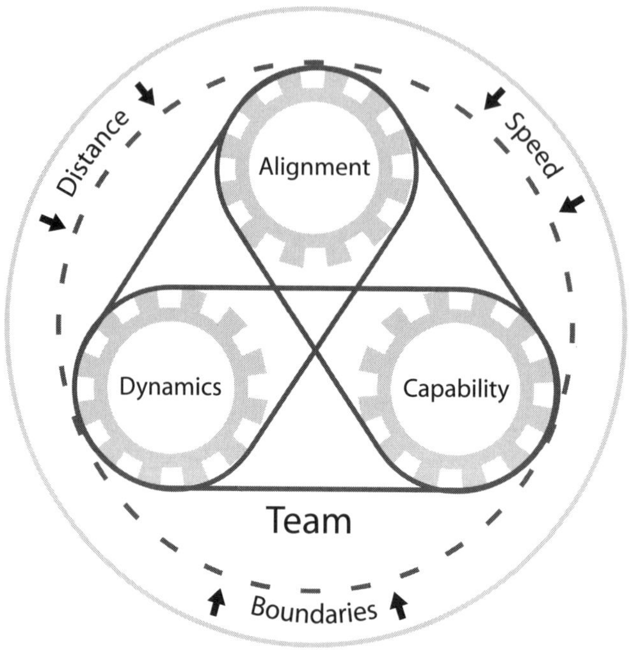

value from the solution has been shortened. This further increases the need to collaborate across different types of boundaries, both functional and organizational, and to move with greater speed than ever before.

In this book, we describe three fundamental, interdependent elements that are critical to a team's performance and results. Managers are responsible for understanding and actively affecting each of the following three elements:

1. Aligning their team's actions to specific purposes
2. Ensuring that the right resources and people are available to the team
3. Managing the team's internal and external relationships

As Figure 1.1 indicates, as managers navigate these fundamental challenges of alignment, capability, and dynamics, they also need to be aware of three factors that will force additional complexity onto these challenges:

1. The *speed* at which their teams will have to form and produce results
2. The *distance* that will separate members
3. The blurred *boundaries* of membership and accountability

We will describe each of these in more detail below, but first let's set the stage with a few basics—what a team is, and what role you, the manager, play.

WHAT IS A TEAM?

The use of teams varies so much across companies that it is difficult to find a single accepted definition of what a team is and how it should work. Sometimes companies use "teams" as an overall philosophy for how to structure work, as in "We're a team-based organization." Sometimes it is a cultural value: "We're all part of the same team," "Be a team player," and "Teamwork is one of our priorities" are common phrases that capture this thought. Although these may be good sentiments, using these phrases may lead to confusion. Some are quite vague and some, such as "team player," can have two meanings—being a team player could mean taking on whatever tasks need to be done to help the team accomplish its set goals, or it could indicate going along with the group opinion to keep harmony rather than offering a different opinion.

What do we really mean when we talk about teams? Below are some general guidelines for what makes a team and what doesn't. A team:

- *Is a small group of people.* Too few or too many and it's difficult to manage or get results. The optimal size depends on the task.
- *Is committed to a shared purpose or goal.* There is a specific reason the team exists and why the members engage with one another.
- *Has complementary skills.* Too much of this and not enough of that can mean core capabilities are missing.

- *Has mutual and individual accountability.* Individuals manage their own work, and also share accountability for the team's results.
- *Works interactively and interdependently.* Individuals rely on each other to meet their objectives instead of trying to get there alone.

Not All Groups Are Teams

Think about a tightly connected performance versus a loose collection of people. A string quartet is a team, but a group of random musicians sitting in on an evening jam session is not. Defense lawyers working on the same case interact differently than lawyers who all work for a large law firm. In each example, individuals can participate on both levels and clearly define the differences–why they're there, how they act, and how others act.

Compared to a group, people on a team have a stronger sense of unified purpose. They have a higher level of commitment. There is greater accountability to the other members and greater amounts of time spent together. There is a personal sense of role and responsibility. By working together, the members of a team each enhance the overall team performance–getting more and better results than they could have accomplished as individuals or perhaps as members of temporary groups. The expectations for positive results are higher for a team than for a group.

Teams Come in Different Flavors

Companies use teams in many ways. There are management teams, set up to move the company forward and address issues in a "big picture" way. Cross-functional teams involving members from different departments who may be used to handle certain tasks or projects. Specific project teams within a company are organized to work on certain tasks and tend to have finite deadlines. Ad hoc teams may be set up to include outside consultants who are hired to work with company employees on certain issues or projects.

How teams work also varies. Some teams have all members co-located and interact on a daily basis. Other teams have some or all of their members geographically dispersed and need to work virtually. Some teams are made up largely of peers, while others have a clearly defined manager to direct and guide their work.

Virtual Teams

Often when we think of teams, we think of people doing something together in the same place at the same time. However, more and more, we have teams of people who work primarily using telecommunications technology. These virtual teams are like *co-located teams in most respects and share the same basic challenges.* Some experts joke, "They're teams, only more so."

There are several challenges that virtual teams face compared to co-located teams. First, they don't tend to interact casually. They don't bump into each other in the hallway, and they are less likely to ask a quick question "in the moment," although the increasing use of instant messaging is helping. Virtual teams also tend to have more structured meetings and conversations.

Second, virtual teams miss the rich nonverbal cues that others offer when face-to-face. Over the phone or via e-mail, we can't see facial expressions or posture or someone doodling in a meeting. You can't see someone wince, smile, shrug, or slouch. Sometimes you can't be sure the person is even there (how many of us have snuck out of a conference call to grab a quick cup of coffee or return a phone call?). As such, a virtual team's communication needs to be more frequent or more direct or more explicit than if the members all were in the same room. Thus, the virtual team mantra: "Talk early, talk often, and share what you know when you know it." Otherwise, the team will quickly devolve into a group.

These two challenges often exacerbate a third challenge: Virtual team members may not share a common culture and sense of community. They may be located in different countries or in different divisions of the company. Their functional group and geographic location typically shapes their identity, language, and perspective. Therefore, members may not understand each other's slang, jargon, or idioms, and they may have different norms or ways of behaving.

On top of these challenges, organizations are employing virtual, cross-functional teams to solve today's complex business issues, yet they have not figured out how to support them well. The team members often have a "home" department or function from which they derive their core identity; are given direction; are measured, trained, and paid; and are provided social support. In these teams, members are expected to manage the tensions of dual citizenship—to the cross-functional team and to their home department. These situations are becoming more prevalent every day, however, the metrics, structure, work processes, and priority systems of most companies have not kept pace.

If we all recognize the potential benefits and agree on the best characteristics of effective teams, why isn't it getting any easier? Although teams can create wonderful results, for various reasons, many groups never gel and become teams. Instead, they spend time thrashing around unproductively and never fulfill the promise or achieve results. Their members may leave the experience with a negative view of teams, perhaps making participation on their next team (which will probably still occur despite their avoidance) even more difficult because of their resistance.

Collaboration takes time and patience. Although the end result is better, the decision-making process may feel slower, the communication and coordination needs may be higher, and, like a high-end sports car, a team may require precision tuning to keep purring and performing well. Whenever people get together, there is potential for friction. Some people can never cede control to others or tuck away their egos long enough to become part of a team. For all these reasons and more, teams can be difficult to create and get the benefits from.

That being said, we see no evidence of companies moving away from teams. Instead, they are continually trying to find ways to make collaboration work more efficiently and effectively. Has anyone discovered a magic formula? Well, no, nothing magic. Each team is unique. Although they may share some characteristics, such as size, composition, structure, and duration, the way team members interact with each other and approach their tasks is distinctive. Yet, there are common characteristics of effective teams and the role the team leader plays.

That's where you, the manager, come in.

THE MANAGER'S ROLE

As the use of teams has evolved and grown in the workplace, the manager's role in building and leading effective teams has also changed. Managers can no longer gather information from the people who work for them and make command decisions that the team must then execute. Nor is it enough to assemble a group of talented, hard-working individuals and expect them to be able to "figure it out." Good intentions and hard work aren't enough to be successful against the more complex and rapidly shifting challenges they face.

When effectively managed, teams can offer the benefits of greater creativity, knowledge, information sharing, and problem-solving styles, along with greater efficiency, support, and commitment. Aligned poorly, missing critical capability, working with poor team dynamics, or managed ineffectively, they instead can result in confusion, delay, "groupthink," low accountability, low morale, and disappointing results.

You may have found yourself as a member on both of these types of teams in the past. Being a member of a team that is functioning well can bring out the best in us–these feelings of belonging, support, commitment, and achievement help us to produce great results. There is a great sense of shared accomplishment and achievement when the team members deliver results beyond what they thought possible. On the other hand, being a member of an ineffective team can be an experience you'd probably like to forget–poor group dynamics, low creativity, confusion, and one or two dominating members will result in less than stellar results.

Today's managers have to take a more active role in enabling their teams' abilities to be effective and to get results. You can do this by ensuring that your team's work has *context and meaning,* that they have the *necessary capabilities and resources* to do the work, that their internal *team dynamics are facilitating* rather than hindering their efforts, and that they are integrated and *working collaboratively with their external environment.*

Aligned with a Purpose

A clear purpose aligned with specific goals tells a team *why* they exist, what the desired results are, and what the required work is. It helps the team's members move in the same direction and reduces the likelihood of wasted effort and confusion. A sense of purpose is like a vision–it's typically compelling, directional, and aspirational, and it helps to create context and meaning for the work that the team is doing.

Leading from the center of the organization, it's your job to ensure that the team's work is aligned with the organization's larger strategy, that they have clear goals and priorities, and that they are well organized around the work at hand. It is up to you to make sure they know how they fit in the larger context, and what others expect of them.

Capabilities and Resources

Teams provide a greater range of expertise, viewpoints, and solutions than individuals can offer alone. During the Renaissance era, an educated person *could* have a wide array of rather deep expertise; after all, there was less knowledge to be an expert in. The phrase "a Renaissance man" connotes someone who knows something about everything–history, science, art, music, literature, languages. With the passage of time and the staggering increase in our collective human knowledge, it is now virtually impossible to be a true Renaissance man. There is too much information to master. However, we can bring together a small set of people who collectively encompass a wide range of experience and knowledge. We can combine talents and expertise and make a "Renaissance team." Given the complexity of many problems, and the interconnected nature of our electronic age, we often need the combined perspective of several people who can align well and resolve an issue.

Your role is to make sure the team has the *right* mix of talent; it's not sufficient just to assign random people to a problem. This is really a discovery process: What does the team need, and what do they have today? Both the manager and the other members need to discover what experience and talent each team member brings to the team.

You need to look ahead as well, and plan how to meet future goals and requirements. As a routine part of the job, a manager must assess the team's current capabilities and consider what will be required to meet the team's goals. The manager must then create the plan for growing or obtaining the talent that will be needed to achieve these results. It is a balancing act, though. A manager has to be aware of and address both individual needs and team needs. You have to keep in mind individual aspirations when matching to the opportunities at hand; and depending on the present work tasks, you must assess what needs the team has across a wide range of things, such as budgets, technology, partnerships, and the like.

Dynamics—Inside the Team

Ultimately, there is work to be done. Team dynamics will determine the environment within which the work happens, and to some extent, the quality of the result. What is it like working on this team? What are the dynamics and the culture? Are the team's interactions helping or hindering its ability to make progress? A manager has to pay attention to whatever might affect the team's ability to work effectively, such as community, norms, coordination, communication, conflict, or expectations. You need to help your team create a culture, routines, and practices that bring out the best in people and lead to great results. You also need to minimize the time and energy spent on things counterproductive to this aim.

Outside the Team

How others view your team is partly a function of how you present your team's work. It is affected by the way your team collaborates (or doesn't) with other teams and outside stakeholders. A team's manager often has a more extensive network than his or her direct reports and can smooth the way for the team; the manager can access information from other sources and get additional assets for the team. You can forge collaborative working relationships outside of the team, with your peers and their teams, and with outside stakeholders and their teams. Part of the challenge is how others see your team and part is finding ways to get the benefits of all those diverse talents instead of just incurring the coordination costs.

TODAY'S SPECIAL CHALLENGES

Teams and their dynamics have been studied and written about extensively over the past several decades. Though much is known about the value of teams and what makes them perform well, it doesn't mean that building and leading a team is easy to do. In fact, the challenges of leading teams today have expanded and the need for good quality leadership has never been greater.

What do managers have to do differently to build and lead effective teams today? In this book, we'll explore the manager's role in creating alignment, building capability, and creating the internal and external team environment. Understanding these areas gives you a sound basis for leading a team to great results.

In addition to the foundation, there are a few special challenges that we reflect on, including speed, distance, and boundaries.

Speed Counts

Teams need to form and perform rapidly. Although there is much advice on how new teams should get organized—create a team charter, discuss and agree to norms, define team expectations and roles—not all teams are new, and none has extensive time to devote to these activities. Some have new members who join an existing team, and other members who exit. Regardless of who is on your team today, you and your team have to hit the ground running. You have to figure out how to get people organized and working productively individually and collectively, and you need to do it quickly.

Distance Complicates

When team members are separated by time, distance, culture, or language, the usual team challenges become exacerbated. Logistics and planning are more difficult when members are located more than 50 meters away, let alone 7 time zones. Different work styles aren't visible or obvious to all team members and may result in mistaken assumptions. Technology failures or using an inefficient technology may delay the team's ability to communicate and make progress. Conflicts can be difficult to resolve without the ability for all to meet face-to-face. Assimilating new members takes longer and requires more thought than if the new person could simply shadow an existing member.

Boundaries Are Blurring

Defining team membership can be complex. There may be a nucleus of core members who also have dotted-line connections to individuals and groups beyond the team's recognized boundary. There may be fringe or temporary members whose primary alignment is with another team, but whose interactions with this team will affect its purpose or goals, its capabilities, and its dynamics. Evolving membership makes it both more challenging and more important that you continually assess and manage team dynamics. Who is a "member" of the team isn't always clear.

This means that leading a team effectively in a modern enterprise requires new perspective, skills, and tools. In the chapters that follow, we show you how to build a strong base, and we provide guidance related to the special challenges that you will face along the way.

CHAPTER TWO

2

WHAT RESULTS DO YOU NEED?

IN THIS CHAPTER

Purpose Begins with Strategy ■ Purpose across Distance and Boundaries ■ Getting Clear on Priorities ■ Goals and Outcomes

If a team exists, there must be a clear reason, a purpose, for its being, right? If a team has all the visible characteristics of other teams—members, regular meetings, a budget, and a leader—and there are no major complaints about its efforts, then it must be making progress and achieving its goals, right? Not necessarily. Even though the value of teams continues to be touted and their use within companies continues to expand, reports from the trenches tell us that teams are not nearly as effective in getting results as they could be.

Do we know why? Teams and their performance in the workplace have been the subject of more studies over the years than we can cite here. The bookshelves are filled with expert "how to" guides, best practices, and details about what works and what doesn't in building, leading, and participating in teams. They offer different approaches and a variety of solutions, but one thing that most of them agree on is that clarity of purpose is a critical success factor shared across high-performing teams. Without a unified (and unifying) purpose, a downward spiral can begin—the members' efforts become splintered or misdirected, results become disappointing, and morale becomes low.

Consider your own organization. Hopefully, you can easily describe your own team's purpose and goals and situate this within your company's strategy. However, when asked about teams in other departments or areas, you may be hard-pressed to provide much more than a vague description. You may find that you are not entirely sure what it is that some of them do, especially if their work has no direct connection to your own group's work. In some cases, you might think the other teams aren't sure what they should do, either.

Are there warning signs that a team is at risk of misdirection? Certainly, a lack of team purpose can manifest itself in several ways: meetings with no obvious outcomes, nonexistent or missed deadlines, incomplete or misaligned results, individuals working predominantly on their own, and a high rate of turnover among team members. Working with others requires people to spend time and effort coordinating—deciding work flow, sharing information, dividing tasks, sorting out schedules. Without a clear purpose or desired results, people are less likely to put forth the required effort.

What is life like on a team without a clear and shared purpose or commitment? It can make you feel as if you are moving in slow motion while the rest of the company speeds past. Take the following example: The calendar shows that the team has a meeting and team members show up (at least in the beginning). There is a leader at the front of the room, but no one submitted any agenda items for the meeting. Any "team updates" are nothing more than individual recitations of projects, many of which don't relate to one another. If the meeting had been cancelled, no one would have felt urgency to reschedule it. There are no pressing demands from customers that require the team to collaborate; any issues are easily handled by one member. In discussing a few of the ongoing projects, not much progress has been made, but it's not a crisis because there aren't any "can't miss" deadlines associated with work; no one feels accountable to the other members, so no one is motivated to focus on those projects. A few people are working on individual projects in an effort to just get something accomplished, but they are reluctant to share any details with the rest of the group lest someone try to help or take pieces of the task away from them. One of the members has requested a transfer to another team. People feel few compelling reasons to come into work each day.

Things are out of kilter, and the team is struggling to produce results. Is any of this sounding familiar? If it does, then you have been part of a nonfunctioning team.

What can the team's leader do to help provide a sense of purpose to a team that is struggling or to maintain alignment for a team that is working well now? What gives a team purpose, and how can the leader create it?

PURPOSE BEGINS WITH STRATEGY

A team's purpose should have a clear line of sight between the team's goals and where the company is headed. Yet research tells us that oftentimes teams are unable to connect their day-to-day work to the organization's larger strategy and direction. In some cases, it has never been articulated in a way that they can connect to. In other cases, it is only partially defined. In still others, strategy changes so rapidly that they find it hard to *stay* connected. That finding isn't surprising if team members are expected to make those connections independently. A team's importance to the company's future should provide its members with a shared identity, purpose, and commitment to get things done. So, if that connection is missing, they may not understand where their work fits. They also may be working on the wrong things and not producing the results that the company needs.

Strategy does not simply trickle down through the ranks and magically have meaning for the regions, teams, or individuals that it reaches. The strategy that people hear in a CEO's presentation or read in the annual report is broadly defined, or what some call the "30,000-foot level." That strategy applies to everyone loosely, but it certainly doesn't mention any team specifically or tell a particular team what they should be focused on and why it's important. Your role is to translate that broad strategy into something that *does* make sense for the team. Then, you help them to connect their own work to the company by achieving the strategic objectives.

Are you prepared to translate the corporate, regional, or functional strategy in a way that creates context and meaning for your team? Take stock of your own knowledge. If you find that there are gaps in what you know or what you understand, take steps to find the answers to those questions first. Read what's available to you–annual reports, shareholder meeting summaries, and the like. Talk to regional or divisional people who can help fill in the gaps. It's up to you to have as much information as possible at hand.

If you already feel comfortable in your own understanding, you need to communicate that to your team in a meaningful way that makes sense for everyone. This doesn't mean you need to take them through an exhaustive overview of every element of the company strategy. That's not efficient, given the complexity and rate at which strategies change today. What you do need to do is help them to understand the parts and pieces where they will play a key role and where the benefits of their efforts will be recognized. Tell them the story of where the company is going and how they are being asked to help. Giving your team that connection also helps them understand the reason for change when changes occur and/or helps them to anticipate and suggest adjustments themselves. As Figure 2.1 depicts, you need to make those connections that align what people are working on to the team's priorities and the larger organizational strategy.

For example, a video game development company's marketing team may be assigned the task of predicting future trends in video game purchasing–what sparks buyers' interests and what the "hot" new trend will be. The team members need to understand the importance of "getting out into the field" and talking with teenagers and college students, a prime market for their products. Although some may balk at establishing dialogues with these adolescents, the manager needs to walk team members through the process, showing them how their work is not frivolous but is the backbone to future product design, development, marketing, and sales. As leader of this project, the manager has to explain to the team how their work fits in with the company's overall strategy of becoming the top video game seller for the upcoming holiday season.

FIGURE 2.1 Aligning Goals

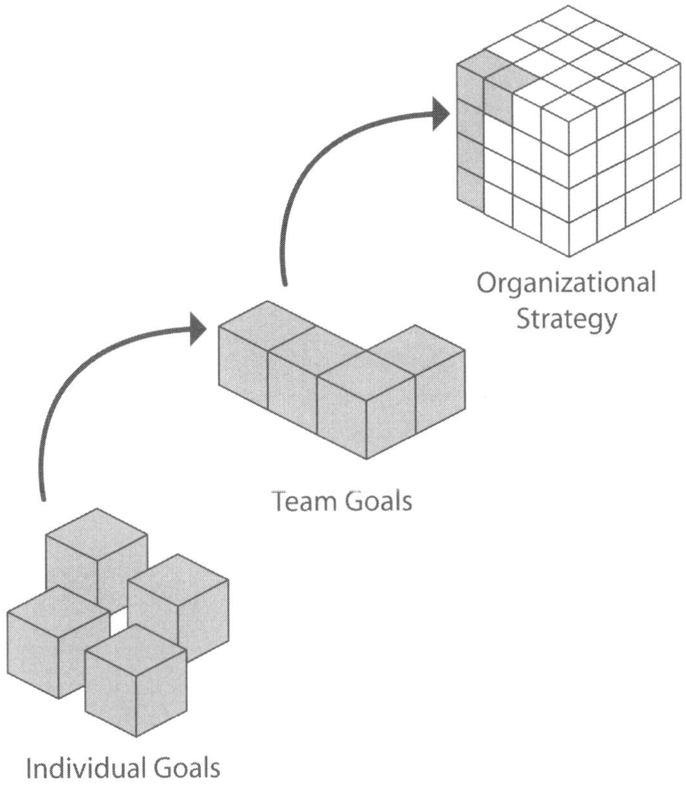

By default, strengthening team members' connections to the company's strategy also makes the connection between their work and other groups more visible. Chances are they will work on related projects or combine efforts when working on larger, more complex tasks. The team can now see the "big picture," and thus the impact and effect that their actions will have on others and their work. Seeing the big picture helps the team make decisions that enable their work but that don't have negative effects elsewhere.

Another benefit is that individual members better understand why the coordinated efforts of all team members will be needed to accomplish the results they want. Remember, the team exists because their tasks are too complex and difficult for individuals to accomplish alone. Shared purpose doesn't mean that team members have to put aside individual interests or preferences or always be in consensus. It does mean that they will use the experience, expertise, diversity, and creativity of all team members to achieve success. They will achieve more together than separately as individuals. As a team, they *can* deliver the "impossible."

Let's take a look at a huge project—the building of a major bridge. We instinctively understand that a few individuals cannot, on their own, set out to build a bridge (unless it's a couple of planks over a creek or something similarly small). Construction of such a project is complicated, involving many groups dedicated to planning and coordinating construction efforts over several years.

The Woodrow Wilson Bridge Replacement over the Potomac River, slated to open its first phase in late 2005 or early 2006, has involved the efforts of many project teams from different agencies and companies. Project crews, such as blasters, concrete teams, trenchers, civil engineers, environmental specialists, and community relations experts, have come together to collaborate on building this bridge, which will alleviate a bottleneck on I-95 and reduce commute times by up to an hour and a half for travelers.

Four agencies, including the Virginia Department of Transportation, the Maryland State Highway Association, the District of Columbia Department of Public Works, and the Federal Highway Administration, also have collaborated on the project. Potomac Crossing Consultants, consisting of team members from Parsons Brinckerhoff, URS Corporation, Rummel Klepper & Kahl, and 13 other active subconsultants, has led the effort and is responsible for the overall bridge project.

The challenge of coordinating this major project and satisfying the requirements of all four agencies has its project manager appreciating his team members. "A big part of my job is coordinating among the various agencies to make sure we're all going in the same direction," said Russ Fuhrman, the joint venture's project manager. "All four agencies have their own day-to-day agendas, and we have to ensure that their needs play into all decisions regarding the project." The decision to make the bridge construction project a joint venture has its benefits. "The joint venture, in conjunction with our clients, did a great job of dividing the project into small contract packages,"

Fuhrman notes, acknowledging that dividing up the job has meant having more interfaces to control. Fuhrman believes the tradeoff has been key to delivering a superior project, on time and under budget. Day-to-day responsibility for the project falls on Construction Manager Jim Ruddell, who is managing 21 major contracts. Said Ruddell, "No one person can run a job of this magnitude. We hire capable people and trust their capacity to make sound judgments and wise decisions." (Walsh, 2004) All the team members are clear on what the goal is and how their piece fits into achieving a successful project. (See our *Translating Strategy into Action* book for more specific tools and examples.)

PURPOSE ACROSS DISTANCE AND BOUNDARIES

When we think about traditional teams, we typically think about examples where membership is fairly stable and team members are in close proximity to one another–for example, a sports team, a response team, or perhaps your own team. These teams have time to build a sense of purpose and commitment; they expect to be together for some time, focused on the same goals. Today, however, these types of teams are more the exception rather than the norm. More common are ad hoc teams that are formed for the completion of a single project, teams whose members are not co-located, or teams whose membership fluctuates as temporary members join them for particular assignments. What are some of the special challenges for creating a shared sense of purpose when one or more team members are separated by time, distance, culture, or primary team affiliation? What about when the team must form quickly and get the job done?

Distance complicates the process. When people are separated by distance, the spontaneity of interaction quickly decreases. Think about the quick questions you call out to those who are near you, the occasional outbursts of communal laughter to someone's response, or even the looks that pass between team members after hearing some news or disconnecting from a client phone call. Having most members co-located while one or more are distributed elsewhere has the potential to create a two-tier membership. Those who are not based in the "main" office or are not a member of the "core team" may feel as if they are not part of the group, and their sense of belonging and sense of shared purpose can suffer as a result. A sense of involvement and community increases the discretionary energy that people put forth—whether emotional, physical, or intellectual—to the team case.

They also may not be able to develop individual relationships with the other members as quickly when they are not co-located or are temporarily assigned. It's not uncommon for virtual or temporary members to perceive bias on the part of the team leader, in favor of those more closely located or those with whom successful working relationships have previously been shared.

You need to pay particular attention to how you address these team members to keep them "in the loop," maintain a greater share of their focus and attention, and keep your project on the front burner in a world of multiple priorities vying for people's time. The ability to understand these challenges and to define and drive a set of routines and work practices that addresses them is the work of a good manager. Consider some of the following suggestions to increase their sense of belonging and alignment with your team's shared purpose:

- Plan for regular one-on-one conversations with all team members. Check in not only about their general reactions to how things are going or their opinions on issues, but also about life, career goals and development, and news.
- Create ample opportunities for both formal and informal contact among team members—one-on-one, small group, or full group.
- Pay attention for signs of conflict. It is easier to deal with a problem early on rather than later. A downside of not being there physically is that there is a greater opportunity to ignore misunderstandings and let issues fester. It is also more challenging to resolve conflict remotely (in many cases). So plan ahead instead of fighting fires.
- Whenever possible, organize face-to-face events for the entire team.

GETTING CLEAR ON PRIORITIES

Even after you've agreed on a purpose and situated your work within the broader strategy, there are always tough choices to be made and tensions to be managed with regards to priorities. How should you direct your time and resources? Where's the leverage? Where's the maximum impact? How do you decide which ones to pursue? How can you help to keep priorities realistic and achievable?

Rather than working simultaneously on too many initiatives, devote most of your time to working on what is most important and where you have the most leverage. Which initiatives, if you complete them, will have the most impact or affect other projects? One way to decide what your priorities should be is to consider how much "bang" you will get out of pursuing a particular path compared to another. Think of it this way: What is the value to the business and how easy or difficult will your goal be to implement? If the goal isn't feasible and the results aren't valuable, you shouldn't spend the time, energy, and money required to do it. If it's impossible to implement, people will get frustrated and the team's time, energy, and money will be wasted.

The team may have to work within paradoxes–balancing things like speed and accuracy–while trying to achieve the desired results. Because they now have a better understanding of the overall strategy and how their goals "fit" within the larger picture, they are in a better position to use their own judgment when the situation requires it.

Too often, the strategic goals get pushed off or postponed when the urgent day-to-day requests start coming in. Teams should now understand the importance of staying focused on their own goals first–after all, other departments are depending on the team's results–and not getting sidetracked by the frequent "urgent" requests. For example, if you have two big tasks and ten small ones, it's easy to get caught up doing the ten small tasks. It's rewarding to cross an item off your to-do list and feel like you made progress. But, once you've eaten away your time on the small stuff, it's hard to find a longer time period and the space needed to tackle something more complex.

Another analogy most of us can identify with is trying to fit everything you need in a suitcase before a trip. Logic tells us (well, most of us anyway) that only so much will fit. So you make sure that the larger or more important items are taken care of first, and then you fill in around the sides and in the gaps with the smaller or more flexible items. That way, you ensure that the most important things aren't left behind. The moral is: If you focus too much energy on the small, "urgent" requests (like socks), you'll be too busy to put significant effort toward strategic objectives (your passport or perhaps your shoes).

GOALS AND OUTCOMES

Once you've created a meaningful connection between your team's purpose and the overall strategy, and have a better idea of the priorities, it becomes easier to define and gain commitment to actual goals and outcomes. It's time to get specific and time to get to work. Not to say that the team hasn't been working hard already; it helps focus effort, though, when you have a guiding target that helps decide what to work on and how, what's a priority and what's not, and what needs to be delivered and at what time.

The acronym SMART is frequently used to describe a framework for thinking about setting goals. Although there are several variations of the acronym in use and the origin is uncertain at this point, the basic guidelines still hold. The common purpose is to give enough definition to your work that you are able to take action.

What characteristics do SMART goals have? Depending on the definition you use, they are specific, measurable, attainable, action-oriented, agreed on, achievable, acceptable, attractive, realistic, relevant, trackable, timely, or tangible. Although there are several variations of the SMART acronym, what they have in common is an attempt to help you write goals with enough detail that you have a vision of what success looks like, understand what you need to do, can measure and track progress, believe that you can do it (although it is not necessarily easy), and have some real target deadlines to drive action.

Let's say a marketing team's goal is to "increase revenue by stimulating more sales." This might sound like a good goal. After all, the team has a measurable task–increase revenue–and a "battle cry"–stimulate more sales. But the goal fails because it is not specific enough. How will the team increase sales? How are sales measured–

by units, by clients, by lots? What is a challenging yet attainable increase in revenue? What is the time framc?

By applying the SMART ideas to the above goal, a better "battle cry" is: "Increase company revenue by 20 percent during the first quarter by selling 25 percent more of existing product to existing clients through incentive programs, and by attracting 20 new major customers for our newest product line." The marketing team now has a graspable action plan and can get to work on achieving that goal.

ALIGNMENT CHECKLIST

- ❑ Connect the work you are doing to a larger strategic purpose.
- ❑ Connect all team members–permanent and temporary, co-located and distributed–with the purpose.
- ❑ Agree on priorities. Where's the leverage? What initiatives will have the most impact?
- ❑ Define goals and outcomes that are specific, measurable, achievable, realistic, and timely.

CHAPTER THREE

3

DO YOU HAVE WHAT YOU NEED?

IN THIS CHAPTER

Building Team Capability ■ Supplying Team Resources ■ Build, Buy, Borrow, or Say No

Your team members understand their role in delivering results for the company and how their work will make a difference. You've outlined some clear goals and objectives and agree on where the top priorities lie. Now, what's required to do the work?

How well does your team's current capability align with the work that you have to do? Do team members have sufficient resources to do the work? Are the goals and objectives challenging for the team? Can temporary members fill the capability gaps that exist? Do the task assignments provide enough opportunity for individuals to grow and develop?

BUILDING TEAM CAPABILITY

One of the benefits of working in teams is that the combined skills and expertise of the full group can be more effective and responsive than the capabilities of individuals alone. We can draw distinct parallels between teams in traditional work settings and specialized teams we observe, such as racing pit crews, ER trauma response teams, or even circus acts. These teams need to act in tight coordination, each specialist understanding and performing his or her part and at the right time. They need to continually practice and improve their skills and techniques, so they can perform smoothly and effectively when called on to do so. Whether observing such teams in real life or on a TV show, we may get caught up in the drama of watching events unfold, and we may not give much thought to the team leader's role in making it all happen.

The managers in these examples are likely facing some of the same challenges that you are: aligning a group of talented individuals around shared goals and outcomes, identifying and getting the resources that the team needs, developing individual skills, helping members coordinate their efforts, and ultimately delivering results for key stakeholders. Although your own tasks may not have the life-changing power that trauma medicine does or might not be as exciting as performing under the big tent, you still will need to build an effective blend of talents for your team. Chances are you have to do it much more quickly than the teams in these examples. You won't have the luxury of "practicing" until you get it right, but instead must transform your group of individuals into a cohesive team quickly.

Duke University's men's basketball coach, Mike Krzyzewski ("Coach K" to most college hoops fans), often speaks of "The Fist." He compares the five players on the court to the fingers on a hand. When pulled together into a fist, the fingers are more effective and powerful than they are individually. Similarly, the players on the court can be much more effective and cohesive acting as a unit than as five individual players. (Krzyzewski, 2001)

Team capability is more than just the sum of individual skills and knowledge, it is about getting the *right* mix of people–understanding the unique competencies that each person brings to the group, matching those people to the right roles, and helping them to work collaboratively. If you have too many people, it's hard to coordinate their efforts. Too few, and there may be too much work or not enough range of expertise for the team to be effective. A barbershop quartet made of four tenors is more limited than one with the standard complement of voices. Having a tenor, lead, baritone, and bass

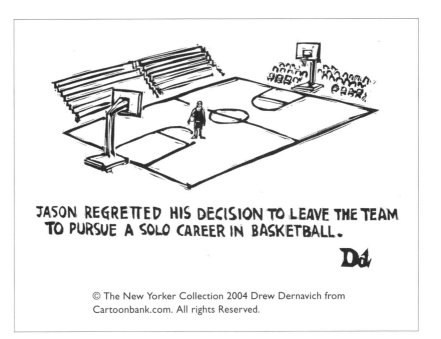

JASON REGRETTED HIS DECISION TO LEAVE THE TEAM TO PURSUE A SOLO CAREER IN BASKETBALL.

allows the quartet to fully execute the music as it was written and arranged. They have the right mix and number of people to meet their team's musical goals. What happens when there are a variety of "extra" members who occasionally fill in for performances? How does the possibility of changing membership affect your ability to create the right mix?

You may be asked to develop a specific team for a specific project. For example, in 2001, Volvo Cars decided to create a concept car designed entirely by women for women. About 20 percent of the company's 28,000 workforce is female, so officials were confident they could pull together an all-female concept car project team. Said Volvo CEO Hans-Olov Olsson at the car's debut, "We're part of an auto industry dominated by men, but wanting to attract a growing group of women car buyers."

The "Your Concept Car" project team of three chief designers and five project managers is believed to be a first in car development. The team of women pooled their skills and created a truly visionary vehicle–one that has dirt-repelling paint, capless filling for gasoline and windshield wiper fluid, a sleek control console, ergonomic seating, extra cargo capacity, and many more woman-friendly features.

The project team made sure to tap the right women with the right skills to create this "dream" vehicle and, although it has yet to be produced, it provided insight into what appeals to women who, as one researcher noted, act alone or have a say in roughly 80 percent of the vehicle purchases in the United States. (Job, 2004)

Define the capabilities that your team will need to be effective. Depending on your clarity of purpose, for some teams this may be an easy exercise, while for others there may be less certainty. This is especially true for newly formed teams, for ad hoc teams, or for established teams who suddenly find themselves in the midst of change–aligning around new strategy, new initiatives, new goals, or new members.

The results you need to achieve and the work to be done drive the capabilities. So start with the type of work that you will have to do. What will this team be focused on? Is this a team whose purpose is to respond to calls for assistance, such as an emergency response team, a hazardous waste disposal team, or a technology help desk, and requires quick thinking and problem-solving skills? Is this primarily a functional team that needs to be very accurate and clear on each person's role and responsibilities, such as a pit crew, a synchronized swimming team, or a military combat unit, in order to execute without incident? Is this more of a creative team charged with developing new products, new slogans, or perhaps new customers? Maybe your team's purpose will require a unique combination of focus.

Look at your team's goals and outcomes that you've identified as priority items. List the combined capabilities–the skills, talents, expertise, backgrounds, and certifications–that you think you'll need to accomplish these goals. Some of the items you identify may be very specific, such as knowing a certain software program or having a professional license or certificate. Other needs may require broader skill sets, such as managing vendor relationships, creative problem solving, preparing budget reports, conflict management, writing proposals, or delivering stakeholder presentations. Depending on the extent of change the new goals bring to the team, existing team members may be able to address many of these challenges, while others may be "stretch goals" for some or all of the members.

What mix of knowledge, skill, and aspiration exists across the team members? Does the current mix address the team's needs? This is about discovery. You and the other team members need to discover what unique competencies and talent each team member brings to the table. In what areas do individuals excel? In what areas do they struggle, and why? When integrated, what does the unique combination mean for the team? As team leader, you're not just pulling people together and saying, "Go." You need to consider how the combination of people matches the outcomes you need to produce.

Discovering individual knowledge, talent, or aspiration for members who work remotely or for members who are primarily assigned to another team or functional unit may require a different approach. Be creative and take the time to incorporate these members into the discovery process.

Consider doing a five-step gap analysis:

1. Describe your team's current set of responsibilities and the tasks that they accomplish now. Note the skills needed to complete these tasks effectively.
2. Describe the set of tasks you think your team will be responsible for a year from now. Note the new skills needed to complete these tasks effectively.
3. Take a "skills inventory" of all team members. Who can do what now? What additional skills or experience do they have?
4. Compare the tasks you spelled out in steps 1 and 2 with the skills your team currently has. Are there any gaps (i.e., tasks that no one is well-equipped to perform)? Do you have appropriate backup for each person; that is, can more than one person on the team perform the more critical tasks?
5. Consider how you may need to adjust your team. Are there areas for development? How quickly does the team need to develop? What capabilities should you consider when seeking new members?

Next, you need to layer in chemistry: How well does your team work together? We will talk about that more in Chapter 4. Keep in mind, though, that the environment that you create for your team's members has a marked effect on their productivity and mood.

Writing about his experiences with the legendary Boston Celtics basketball team, Bill Russell described the team members as a team of specialists, both by design and by talent. He noted, "Like any team of specialists in any field, our performance depended both on individual excellence and on how we worked together. None of us had to strain to understand [that] we had to complement each others' specialties; it was simply a fact, and we all tried to figure out ways to make our combination more effective." (Russell, 1979) You must be sure that the right number and mix of specialists is on your team, and then help them figure out ways to make themselves more effective.

Do people understand and are they comfortable with the tasks or responsibilities that they've been assigned? Whether asked to do more, something slightly different, or something vastly more challenging, people have to understand and be comfortable with the change. It needs to be clear if it is a temporary request, such as "Can you take on this responsibility just for the next few weeks," or if it is more long term, such as "Cheryl is leaving the company and we need for you to pick up all of her clients because we won't be hiring a replacement right away."

Consider the individual's current situation and future aspirations. One person might view the change as a growth opportunity, while another might view it as a side step in relation to where he or she wants to go. This may be difficult at times, because even though a team has a shared purpose and priorities, ultimately it is made up of individual talents, egos, and aspirations. There is an old adage that "There is no 'I' in team." Maybe not, but there is a "me," and people want to understand what team goals, changes, and roles and responsibilities mean for them personally.

Since 1982, the National Basketball Association (NBA) has awarded the 6th Man of the Year Award. The "sixth man" is the first person off the bench to relieve one of the starting five. On any other team, this person would almost certainly be a starter; but on this team, at this point in time, he has been asked to fill a different role. It's a role that he may not have been accustomed to and one that he might resent fulfilling because it's a step down from his usual "starting" position. You might expect the names of those who've received this award to be relative unknowns. In reality, many of the winners were regular starters and stars for much of their careers. They include legendary NBA Hall of Fame inductees, players such as Bobby Jones, Bill Walton, and Kevin McHale.

Do aspirations meet opportunities? Take the time to find out what team members' personal aspirations and goals are. Tapping into what they care about as well as what they are currently good at unleashes capability and discretionary effort. What are their career and life goals, and where are their priorities? Are they new in their current role and want to remain there for some time? Can they assume greater responsibility as a way of developing in their current role? Are there more senior positions within the team or company that they would like to develop into eventually? Don't make assumptions about people. Even if you consider them quite an expert in their current role, they may have other preferences or priorities. Begin a conversation with them.

Consider how their plans map against the team's current and future needs. If your analysis of current versus future needs has revealed some gaps in the team's capabilities, are there individuals who have indicated they would like to develop additional skills in those areas?

Based on where they are today—their aspirations, strengths, and challenges—and the firm's future needs, what growth opportunities can you provide? Think about whether you can address some of their development needs by providing coaching, mentoring, or other opportunities. For example, are there external training offerings that they would benefit from? Are there other projects where they could "shadow" someone who is more proficient at the skills they are trying to improve? Are there smaller projects that would offer a safe environment for practicing some of the skills they want to develop?

What about members who are not part of the team nucleus, such as those who are not active team members or who are assigned temporarily for a particular purpose. What benefits can they derive from being a member of this team? How can this project help them develop?

Be sure to plan for both short-term and long-term resource needs. You may need to ask members to fill a "sixth man" role today while still continuing to develop and work toward another role that they prefer more.

SUPPLYING TEAM RESOURCES

Teams will need access to a set of core resources and support to work effectively. When we mention resources, you may immediately think "budget." Although many of the resources may require spending money, there may be a wide array of resources you can use or claim as a member of the broader organization.

Depending on the nature of the project, teams frequently find that there are technologies available that will make their work easier. People working in very technical areas might require upgrades to hardware components, new software releases, or specialized equipment. Communications tools, such as high-speed Internet access, international cell phones, or video conferencing, may also facilitate the team's work.

Resources can include access to information. Access to some resources (especially those external to the company) may require purchased subscriptions or membership fees to research databases, executive summaries, analysts' reports, news services, or trade publications. You may find that online publications are more efficient for sharing news and updates than a printed version that arrives in the mail. Evaluate what information would be most helpful to the team and how best to acquire it.

Access to internal information resources may be a critical success factor for your team. Sometimes information is tightly held within a company and may require some level of permission in order to get the right information. For example, data that could be helpful to the team's work may be restricted by department or job grade, such as financial data, clinical trial results, customer satisfaction surveys, or product failure analysis. Have you considered how you can remove or work within these access barriers?

Information is not just data across columns and rows, but it is also knowledge and expertise–the discoveries, best practices, and innovative approaches that are happening across the organization. In your role as manager, you are more likely to have begun building a network of connections across the company. You need to regularly interact with others to tap into the "collective wisdom." You probably have relationships with other groups who do similar or related work. Setting up routines for yourself and your team that let you share what you're doing and learn what others are doing can save you time and energy down the road.

For example, a small company had several sales teams, each responsible for a set of clients and regions. Each one created its own sales process, its own supporting materials, and its own way of monitoring calls and expenses. Some teams were more effective and more organized than others. These teams stayed on top of client concerns, communicated well with manufacturing to understand delivery times, and made accounting very happy with their orderly and prompt reports. The other teams could have benefited greatly by adopting processes from a more successful team, but they didn't take the time to learn, and instead stayed with their idiosyncratic and inefficient patterns.

The previous example shows how failure to create a mechanism for knowledge sharing can make teams less efficient, and that such a failure also could diminish your results. A case in point: At Hyde Tools, a $50 million hand-tool company in Southbridge, Massachusetts, the shop floor was reorganized into teams during the mid-1990s to increase productivity and profits. Everyone in the tool plant went through training and began working in teams. Productivity increased dramatically–products that took 15 weeks to go from start to finish before teams were implemented now were being completed in 3 to 4 weeks. While these results were phenomenal on the shop floor, the purchasing and finance departments were unable to keep up, because they weren't prepared for the increased pace or production. Said Dick Ayers, their Human Resources director, "We got the product out the door before they (accounting and finance) could process the paperwork." (Fenn, 1995) Had the purchasing and finance departments been aware of the shift to teams and expected an increase in throughput, they might have been prepared for the shop-floor teams' impact on them.

There is an old adage that says, "A wise man learns from others' mistakes; a fool, his own." Similarly, why reinvent the wheel? Information is a critical resource that can keep you from duplicating efforts and duplicating mistakes. By analyzing past successes and failures, you can help your team members make their work even better. Part of your job is to build and maintain relationships so that you have access to information as you need it.

You also should encourage your team's members to build their own ties to others inside and outside the company. One advantage of a team is the availability of multiple perspectives. Each member encounters a different set of people in the course of his or her day, which allows for much greater access to information, news, rumors, and advice than you could get on your own. Help your team's members learn how to leverage their own ties.

What about those members who operate primarily outside the nucleus of the team? Some may have been added to the team because of the experience and capability they lend, but you also should make sure that they have the resources they need to work effectively. Are they lacking any resources that are readily available to the rest of the team?

Those who are located at a central "home base" location may take certain resources for granted. Virtual team members may not have as quick an access to company resources, such as accounting, human resources, or subject matter experts. For example, in a small, newly opened satellite office, people frequently find themselves without any direct information technology support. Expecting these folks to follow your last minute instructions on connecting a new piece of equipment just prior to a meeting can be a cause for disaster.

Do external members have special needs in terms of resources? Depending on their location and the nature of their work, they may have any number of requirements that others do not. Translation services, professional printing services (no color printer on site), contracted secretarial support, and an international cell phone are a few examples of specific needs off-site workers may have. They also may need a larger budget for items such as travel expenses, telephone bills, and the like.

What steps can you, as manager, take to help build off-site workers' network of capabilities and resources within their own region?

BUILD, BUY, BORROW, OR SAY NO

How will you close the gaps between what you have—the capabilities, technologies, funding, expertise, and information—and what you need? You have to develop a plan for acquiring what your team will need—both now and in the future. Will you build, buy, or borrow what you need? You may find that you can creatively use all three methods.

Ultimately, the team is more efficient if you can develop existing capability within its configuration. Keep in mind that people don't leap from having no capability in an area to the mastery level overnight; and not everyone will want or need to develop to the same degree. Like martial arts students who develop through the many levels of colored belts, members of your team will have different levels of competency. Some will have only a passing proficiency and no desire to develop further, and that may be all you need. Others will be more experienced and want to become even more advanced to the point that they can mentor others. When planning development, consider the level of competency you actually need. It may not be efficient to have too many experts in a particular area.

Explore a variety of ways to help people develop. Some competencies are best learned through organized training while others are best learned through on the job "learn by doing." For example, if a team member needs to develop a technical skill and is beginning with very little knowledge, training classes may be more effective for this person than trying to plod through a manual.

Other competencies, such as client relationship management or business development, may be very specific to your business and best developed through coaching and practice with more senior people. Who on the team, or perhaps on another team, would be able to assume the role of coach for developing this competency in others? Is this a common need among teams, and thus offers some opportunities to work collaboratively on the problem? Once in a "training mode," are there "safe" opportunities for practicing their new skills where they can receive feedback without fear of failure? Perhaps they could shadow a coworker with a longstanding customer who will be more forgiving if minor mistakes are made.

Development takes time, and choosing to build may still leave you with a gap for some period of time. You may be able to borrow resources or capabilities from within the organization to temporarily close the gaps that you have. If your gap is in a particular competency, perhaps someone who is more skilled and experienced could temporarily join your team—to both address your current needs and to help the rest of your team develop more quickly. But be careful. Brooks's Law (Brooks, 1975)—"*Adding manpower to a late software project makes it later*"—may have been referring to software development projects, but it can easily apply to many other situations. Adding people is not always the best solution.

Borrowing internal capability or resources may not actually be free, because it could have some associated costs. You may owe a debt to the team (especially the team's leader) who loaned the resource and they will expect you to return the favor. You may have to cover a portion of someone's salary for the period of time that he or she is assigned to your team. You may even be asked to chip in to cover your share of the cost of a purchased tool or technology.

There are also instances where you need to buy the capability or resource required. Perhaps you simply can't devote the time necessary to build the capability internally—you need it right away. Maybe the technology or expertise is so new that there is no place within the organization from which to borrow it. Then again, the new tool could save your team so much time and energy that it's just worth it.

Consultants are one example of a resource a team may need to "buy." Consider the case of bank mergers and acquisitions. Let's say Apex Bank's merger team—made up of top strategy, finance, analysts, corporate communications, marketing, branding, and other key players—is focused on moving forward with top-secret negotiations to buy TopBank. As part of his role on the merger team, Bob, the head of corporate communications for Apex, must begin planning for the merger announcement. He could send members from his corporate communications team into the city where their merger target is headquartered, but the media may be watching closely, and maintaining the secret is of utmost importance (if the merger falls through, then none will be the wiser).

Bob determines the best course of action to keep the merger a secret is to hire a public relations (PR) firm. The outside firm can send one of their high-level representatives to set up arrangements for the international media event. Cathy, the PR rep, must sign a strict letter of confidentiality, with severe financial punishments for leaking the information. Then, with the stipulation that Cathy uses "neutral" credit cards to deflect any interest in the bank and that she make no reference to the bank, Cathy must proceed with making arrangements for a major media event using a cover story. If the merger is a "go," Bob and his Apex Bank corporate communications team will fly into TopBank's city and proceed with rolling out the media plan. If the merger fails, Bob will call Cathy and give the word: "You have two hours to cancel everything."

In this example, buying the consultant's time and expertise in setting up large events in distant cities makes the most sense for the situation. If a number of Apex Bank's corporate communications' team members were to head into TopBank's territory, it might raise suspicions.

When major league baseball announced that Denver, Colorado, and Miami, Florida, had been granted expansion teams that would begin play in 1993, Commissioner Fay Vincent had to determine what resources those expansion teams would receive. For the first time in history, the Commissioner declared that leagues were required to share expansion revenue and provide players for the expansion draft. The American League would receive $42 million of the National League's $190 million in expansion revenue, and they would have to offer a number of players in the expansion draft.

When they expanded again in 1998, the two new teams received a total of $155 million in expansion fees over a five-year period. The draft pool included not only all players on the current teams' 40-man rosters, but anyone in their organization who had been drafted in 1994 or earlier. The expansion teams would draft 35 players, but existing teams could protect 15 players from the draft pool in the first round. The two new teams were able to assemble a mixture of seasoned veterans and newly developing talent.

You may be asked to organize a new team but are limited in terms of whom and how many people you can select from within the organization. If you are forming a completely new team, in addition to the capabilities of individuals don't forget to think about:

- *Size.* Too many and it becomes unmanageable, too few and you can't complete the work.
- *Diversity.* Avoid the tendency to hire people who are just like you. Consider a diversity of background, experience, gender, race, age, and the like.
- *Community.* How will the individuals fit and work together as group?
- *Cost.* You still have a budget and have to consider the price tag.

How will the team continue making progress while you are working on building, borrowing, or buying capabilities and resources? One way is to set expectations and agree to an appropriate amount of work it has to do. Be clear on what your team can do and by when. Not everything has to be done as requested. Negotiate to meet the real need, and in a way that works for your team.

One of the great things about having a strategy and clear priorities is that it brings focus. Another is that it circumscribes what you will do and helps inform what you will not do. As the team leader, it is imperative that you understand the priorities and learn how to say no to certain things. When someone asks your team to take on a new project during your busiest time, and your gut wrenches thinking about what it means to your team and the results you've promised, you may need to say no. At a minimum, you certainly need to explore alternatives in terms of deliverables, time frames, and other partners to help out; or you may need to renegotiate priorities. In either case, saying yes when you feel no isn't the right thing to do. It may put your team in a bind and ultimately put the deliverables in jeopardy. Get comfortable with exploring alternative pathways to saying yes or saying no. Be strategic in what your team works on. If it's outside your priorities, or outside your team's abilities, you probably shouldn't agree to work on it.

CAPABILITIES CHECKLIST

- ❑ Get clear on the work to be done to achieve the goals set forth.
- ❑ Complete a gap analysis of the capabilities and resources your team will need in the future versus what they have today.
- ❑ Inquire into and understand your team members' aspirations as well as their current skills and talents.
- ❑ Make sure you continue to monitor the strategic direction of the company and align your group accordingly. Recognize that things will change.
- ❑ Determine your priorities, and make smart choices. Make sure that lots of non urgent, low-priority requests don't affect your ability to address the high-priority items.
- ❑ Scope the work to match the capacity and capabilities you have available now—occasionally having to say no doesn't have to mean no. Perhaps instead it means:
  - *Negotiating the work:* Can we do this much rather than the whole thing?
  - *Negotiating the milestones:* Can we talk about how we stage and sequence the work and deliverables?
  - *Finding alternatives:* Would this work just as well?
  - *Finding partners:* We can do it if some of your staff can help out.

CHAPTER FOUR

4

HOW WILL YOU WORK AS A TEAM?

IN THIS CHAPTER

Managers Have Multiple Points of Focus ■ Setting Expectations ■ Agreeing to Norms ■ Keeping Everyone Connected ■ Managing Day-to-Day

Today, managers are often player-coaches. As a player, they are part of the team, working alongside the other members on the same goals and objectives. As a coach, they are working to enable the team's success–assessing current capabilities, assembling key resources, and creating the right environment–and are interacting with those who affect the team (e.g., the equivalent of referees, other team coaches, and league administrators). They are simultaneously a part of the team and apart from the team.

In these next chapters, we are going to examine the two sides of managing a team: looking inside at the dynamics occurring within the team itself, and then looking outward to how the team interacts with its external environment. Both can affect the team's ability to work effectively and get the results they want. Teams today are often expected to form and produce results right away, making managing the team dynamics both more challenging and more important. It may be tempting to bypass addressing team dynamics altogether in your eagerness to get started, because discussing team norms and expectations can seem like a waste of time, especially to seasoned workers. You might not schedule a two-day retreat, but don't ignore dynamics altogether. Be creative and work quickly to set expectations, establish norms, and keep people aligned.

MANAGERS HAVE MULTIPLE POINTS OF FOCUS

As a manager of a work team or a manager of other managers, you set the tone, shape the goals, and may distribute work among team members. Your role involves monitoring the team's results as well as their interactions. You need to ensure that the individuals are performing well, while at the same time ensure that the team is meeting its collective goals.

There are many books that explore team dynamics and organizations that help teams improve their interactions. Some talk about what roles people should play, such as Meredith Belbin's taxonomy, which proposed roles such as coordinator, implementer, and plant (idea generator). Some people naturally gravitate to certain roles or functions relating to task or process. The idea is that if a team has assembled people with complementary skills or focus, they will have a "complete team" that can meet its goals. These ideas are about the interplay of members' skills. (Belbin, 1993)

Other books, and some organizations, focus on the interplay of team members' personalities and styles. They focus on how to build esprit-de-corps. For example, Action Learning Associates provides a one-day course for teams where members have to perform unique problem-solving tasks, cooperative physical tasks, and trust-based tasks. Throughout the day, team members have to process how they are performing and interacting, that is, how their personal styles play out in the activities they're doing. By the end of the experience, they have gained some insight into behavioral patterns in the team, and their effect on results.

Another way of organizing "personalities" relies on the function of the person to the team, separating them into four types: the action-oriented, the analytical, the administrative, and the visionary. Pros and cons exist for each type. For example, the action-oriented team member wants to get started on the project, but may push forward too soon, before all of the information is gathered. The analytical team member is great at gathering and processing information, but may take too long to leap into the project. The administrative team member will keep the team on schedule, but may get bogged down in specifics. And the visionary team member may supply a great "big-picture" vision of where the team wants to go, but may be unable to take the specific steps to get there. (Weiss, 2002) *Knowing how your team members function will help you guide them toward your team's goal.*

A third method focuses on the common pitfalls of teams. For example, Irving Janis's work on "groupthink" explores the decision-making failures of highly cohesive teams. The need to conform leads members to censor themselves. They withhold doubts or information that contradicts the thrust of a conversation. (Janis, 1971) Others highlight pitfalls that may arise from too much divergence; people don't agree on what they need to do, they squabble, or they have completely different work processes.

All of these are aspects of managing a team. Managers need to focus on the internal team dynamics and continue to use other core management skills. You must be sure you have the right mix of people, that you have set clear expectations and goals, and that the team finds ways to work together productively and generatively.

SETTING EXPECTATIONS

Few people like surprises, especially nasty ones. As a manager, you want to avoid being surprised by bad news. As a team member, you probably wouldn't want to be surprised by the message that you've been doing the wrong thing. Simply put, people need a clear idea of what's expected of them, so they can put their energy where it will be well received. You must set the tone, shape the goals, and clarify the tasks that your team needs to do, individually and collectively. You are directing attention and then evaluating how well people did.

This can start at a basic level. One manager at a major pharmaceutical company knew that she needed to reinvigorate her team's meetings, so she used a simple technique to stimulate discussion between team members. She opened up her next meeting by asking members how she, in her role as team leader, could ensure the meetings would be dull and worthless. Team members had plenty of experience with such meetings, and quickly offered a number of ways to guarantee a lackluster, low-energy meeting. This exercise was taken seriously; a list was created, giving the manager a clear idea of what to steer clear of in future meetings. She quipped, "With this list, I then had a pretty clear idea of what to avoid. When you see all the things that can go wrong it can become very clear what to do instead, and I immediately realized there were a hundred ways I could go about enlivening these meetings. This included thinking about the environment, finding ways to engage people, sharing responsibility, and giving everyone a voice. It's absolutely no surprise that this one simple technique has helped to transform the energy we have in these meetings." (Lewis, 2004)

For individual members, you need to work with them to understand their role and what their outputs are. At one company, communication between team members and the manager was messy—the manager would get e-mail updates from some team members, phone messages from another, and scraps of paper from yet others. What resulted was chaos, and he couldn't be sure he had the latest information on a project, because a scrap of paper could have slipped off his desk or an e-mail could be buried in his inbox. This manager knew that for his team to proceed effectively, a simple, consistent communication process had to be established. The manager took the step to outline how he expected team members to leave messages and updates, paving the way for smooth communications in the future.

For the team, you need to be clear on what they need to accomplish, by when, and why. Effective managers convey expectations on a regular basis, not just on special occasions (like at a team retreat or at a quarterly meeting). Some managers build routines that help them, such as a weekly meeting or a quick catch-up at the start of each day. They use these opportunities to remind the team of its purpose, inform them of any changes in the broader organization, and to reinforce expectations.

It's not enough just to set expectations; people need to be able to see how closely they are meeting those expectations. You must think about what you measure. Just by measuring something you send a signal that it's important and that you are paying attention to it. For example, you may track your team members' attendance at regular meetings–this may be your way of gauging members' dedication to the task. If so, make this clear up front. You're more likely to have good attendance at meetings if your team understands this. Your choice of what to measure has symbolic weight. Do you only evaluate individual performance or is there a team component as well? In our above example, is it important to you that every person working on a specific task for the overall project attends the meeting, or is one person from that task force sufficient?

Similarly, managers must consider how to distribute accountability. Which tasks are truly individual tasks (i.e., they are assigned to a specific person)? Which tasks are they collectively responsible for? Do temporary members share the same level of accountability and success as the core team? This, too, is a set of expectations you'll need to establish.

Measures and accountability help people understand where to focus their attention and energy; managers also can use rewards to reinforce what's expected and when it has been achieved. Rewards, like measures, have both a tangible and a symbolic effect. For example, if you have been stressing teamwork, and then give rewards based only on individual performance outcomes, you have just undermined your own message.

Take the case of a restaurant team. Let's say the restaurant operates on a "group tip" basis, meaning all tips are combined and divided between staff at the end of the night. The chef, sous chef, kitchen staff, maitre d', wait staff, bartender, wine steward, and bus boy all contribute to a patron's experience in the restaurant. On a particularly hectic night, one of your waiters goes above and beyond duty in serving guests. If you, as manager, single out this waiter with a more generous tip on this night compared with the others, you've undermined the "all for one, one for all" spirit you've worked to create. Think of a better way to commend the waiter. For example, a well-placed comment on this waiter's team spirit at the next day's prep meeting could encourage the team as a whole.

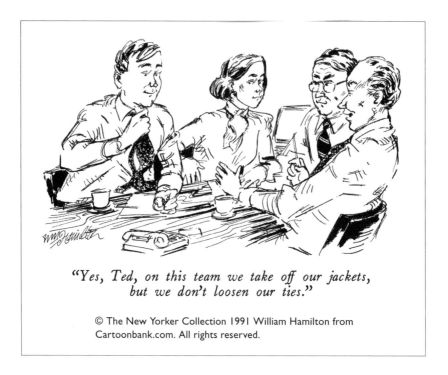

"Yes, Ted, on this team we take off our jackets, but we don't loosen our ties."

AGREEING TO NORMS

Earlier in this chapter, we mentioned that managers need to set a tone for the team and help them work effectively and efficiently. We just discussed setting expectations as one way to do so. Another aspect to consider is the group's norms. Norms are the (informal) rules or shared values that guide a group's interaction on several levels. Norms may define how the members will coexist in a shared space and how they want to work together as a team. They are the operating rules that have developed over time and that team members have agreed to (implicitly or explicitly). They can focus on what the team wants to do (such as how to handle certain situations), or they can focus on what the team wants *not* to do, or what they want to avoid.

Norms also can vary in degrees of subtlety, to the degree that it may be difficult for new or occasional members to discover all the unstated rules of the team environment. Sometimes they can be so subtle that even existing team members aren't completely aware of them—that is, until they're broken.

Norms can vary in level of importance to team members and can generate different levels of reaction when broken. For example, the team may have a norm that whoever takes the last cup of coffee should brew a new pot and not leave behind an empty pot. If this norm is broken, the non-coffee drinkers probably wouldn't even notice; however, the coffee drinkers who depend on a cup a few minutes after getting to work can get very upset—especially if they think one team member is the regular culprit. Something as simple as this can lead to resentment and could threaten the team's future performance if not addressed.

Subtle or Unstated Norms

- We will be honest with one another.
- It's okay to "dress down" when no visitors are expected.
- If you make a mess, pick it up.
- We prefer not to talk about work items during lunch breaks—that's our personal time.
- If one of us can't keep a commitment, that person will let someone know right away.
- If one of us sees a problem that others haven't noticed, he or she will bring it to someone's attention.
- When you have a problem that's proving difficult to solve, it's okay to grab a couple of coworkers and have an informal brainstorming session, rather than continuing to work on your own.
- Our manager will hear about a problem from a team member first, rather than from an external source.

More Explicit Norms

- We start and end meetings on time, as scheduled. Think Swiss: 10 AM means 10:00:00 AM.
- We will not take other calls, answer pages, or check e-mail during meetings.
- We will listen and not interrupt when someone else is talking.
- The meeting organizer will distribute an agenda and material at least 36 hours before the meeting.
- For each meeting, someone will volunteer to take notes and send the minutes out within three days of the meeting.
- We expect each team member to answer e-mail and voice-mail messages within 48 hours.
- Quarterly meetings are important and everyone should arrange their schedule in order to attend.

Norms often define how a team wants to handle certain situations. Ideally, a team discusses them before events occur, so that people know how to respond and how to expect others to respond. Some teams have formal meetings to agree on their norms, and creating a team charter is one way to establish them. Others allow norms to evolve gradually, by trial, error, and feedback. Because they've been stated or tested, if team members feel others haven't adhered to the norms, there is more freedom to raise the issue: "We agreed to respond to e-mails within 24 hours. This is the third time you have waited more than four days to respond. Is something happening with you that we should know about?"

If teams haven't discussed how to handle a particular situation before it happens, you can still use the event as an opportunity to discuss what to do in the future. Rather than focusing on blame for the present, talk about how you want it to be different the next time around. Too many times, we fail to take advantage of the opportunity to explore a misstep.

Setting norms as a team activity gives team members a chance to define what's important to them and to learn more about what's important to the other team members. One person may care greatly that meetings start on time. Another may hate being interrupted when speaking. A third may need to see an agenda in advance, to be able to think about any issues he or she may need to speak about. All these individual concerns and preferences form the basis for the team norms. Members often create norms around how to ask or offer help, how they will make decisions, how they intend to resolve conflict, and how they would prefer to communicate (frequency and medium).

As a team manager, you need to monitor how well the norms are working, look for natural forces at play, and help the team adjust them as needed. Some team dynamics will be beneficial to the team, and some will not. If you see bad patterns developing between members or suspect that conflict is about to erupt, it is likely your role to intercede and help them reshape their interactions. Should your goal be to have a team with no conflict? No. Good conflict—challenging each others ideas or approaches to a problem—can help the team members learn from one another and find the best solutions.

But disagreements on issues that aren't related to work, such as personal or social issues, are not productive. In these cases, it is usually best to make a preemptive strike before the issue escalates. Structure a time, place, and format for dealing with the issue now instead of after the fact.

Managers have been known to say, "I feel like a parent jumping into a sibling squabble. I thought these people were adults! But here they are, arguing over XYZ, like a bunch of ten year olds." To the extent that their squabbles are disruptive to the team getting its work done, you may need to mediate, and like sibling squabbles, the underlying issue may not be XYZ. It is your role to guide the team in identifying the cause of the discord and enabling them to get back on track.

KEEPING EVERYONE CONNECTED

Communication forms the basis for human relationships. You communicate with people throughout the day: one-on-one, in meetings, on the phone, via e-mail, or through more formal channels. You likely speak with your peers about their groups' outputs or common issues. You update your manager on how various projects or outputs are progressing. You chat with your direct reports about their tasks, concerns, and needs. You might speak to customers or suppliers, coordinating when materials or deliverables will arrive or ship. In the context of an organization and in a team, communication is a core coordination mechanism. At the end of a typical day, you may feel as if all you have done that day is talk–but that talk is crucial in aligning the team's activities.

Other books in the Leading from the Center series (see *Influencing and Collaborating for Results*) talk at length about how to craft and communicate an effective message. For coordination purposes, it helps to have two or three specific guiding messages. These messages tie the work the team is doing to the overall strategy. They help explain why the team is doing what it is doing and keep people focused on the few critical tasks.

Once you have a few core messages, you need to deliver them to the team regularly and without fail. Don't tell one person something that contradicts what you told another person. Keeping messages consistent is especially important. As manager, if you have stressed the importance of weekly written progress reports yet let one particular team member "skip" the updates, you're undermining the team's performance and sending the subtle message that the reports aren't important, when in fact, they are. Similarly, if you hear a team member relaying the wrong message, you need to correct the misperception.

It's not enough for you to communicate well; members need to communicate among themselves. You need to help the team coordinate their actions and flag issues before they grow unmanageable. Consider the following about your team:

- Have they developed routines around sharing information?
- Do they have a comfortable and effective way to ask for input?
- If someone gets irritated, is there a way to handle the conflict well?

What we've noted so far is communicating around practical matters: when the meeting is, was their part of the report finished, was a mess left by the first shift for the second shift, or when the new specs are scheduled to arrive.

Communication is critical to teams for other reasons as well. *It is the primary way we establish rapport and negotiate our working relationships.* We use communication mechanisms to create a shared work environment. Think about different teams that you've been a part of. Some leaders may have been serious and task-focused. Others may have used humor to "lighten up" the interactions and work. Some may have said (in word and deed) that they "are collaborative and succeed and fail as a team." Another might have created a competitive environment. Leaders can be effective with an all-business attitude or by showing interest and discussing what people do outside of work.

Compare two managers. The first comes in every morning and walks around and talks to the team, asking people how their evening was, informally catching up on the team's work, and getting a read on any potential problems. These chats are sometimes one-on-one, other times a few other team members may wander over and join in. The second manager sets up formal one-on-one meetings each week with each team member, ostensibly to review what the team member has accomplished that week and to review plans for upcoming week. The manager refuses to let anyone work remotely (even though the company encourages people to do so), saying, "How will I know you're actually working if you're not here?" Anytime the manager walks the halls, it takes the form of popping around corners, interjecting himself or herself into team members' discussions, and then telling them to get back to work. Their reaction? The team actively avoids this manager, provides minimal information, and only speaks among themselves if the manager is away from their immediate work area.

Both managers want to accomplish the same things: monitor the work the team members are doing, identify any problems, balance workloads across the team, and make sure the team is hitting its deadlines. However, the way the two communicate with their teams is drastically different. The first engenders trust and collaboration, the second paranoia. Their styles create dramatically different environments.

In leading a team, you probably want one who trusts one another and you, who will communicate openly, and who will provide feedback. Otherwise, all you have created is a group of individual contributors working independently, not an integrated team.

Does It Matter How a Team Interacts?

It matters greatly how a team interacts. If a team is unable to coordinate their efforts, they waste time, effort, money, and motivation. Frustration and exasperation are not good morale boosters. Second, if a team can't communicate effectively, they lose time and energy on conflict, misunderstandings, and errors. Again, this isn't the result you want as a manager. Finally, people need to feel a part of the group. As social animals, people have a need to affiliate with others and to feel they belong. At the same time, they have a need for fairness and to feel that others are also working equally hard.

MANAGING DAY-TO-DAY

The Situation

David sat heavily in his desk chair and stared out the window. As Global Marketing Manager for MCM Corporation, he was responsible for the worldwide launch of the company's newest product, a Virtual Conference Room, but his team was stumbling–and he needed to figure out what to do.

His team's task was to coordinate the marketing and ad campaigns in seven regions around the world. A year ago, David had personally selected each team member for work on a different campaign, and assigned each a specific geographic area. That launch had been a huge success, largely because the team had worked beautifully together. The company even awarded them bonuses. With that history, David and the team felt confident about taking on this new challenge.

The team knew from the start that having a consistent message would be critical to gaining market share and establishing their product as the industry standard. They began doing focus groups on potential advertising tag lines to see which one had a universal appeal.

The "Bobbseys," otherwise known as Roberto and Bob, took charge of the marketing research. They worked well together (almost too well) and were very experienced marketers in regions where MCM had a strong presence. They had been updating the others every ten days or so, at the team's regular meetings. The data returned from the Americas, Europe, and the Middle East had been positive; Eastern Europe and Australia/New Zealand were mixed. Although the Bobbseys had missed the deadline for finishing the research, no one said anything and just let them continue to gather data.

Marcie, who had wowed the team with her insight and creativity, had been uncharacteristically quiet lately. Her responses to questions were terse, to the point, and flat. Her body language screamed "I don't want to be here." As the weeks progressed, the tension between Marcie and the others intensified. It seemed that she now would only respond to David's questions, and even then, reluctantly. Her territory—Asia—was an especially sensitive one for the company; it was a critical market and there were rumors that a competitor was prototyping a similar product. When David asked Marcie if everything was okay, she replied that Roberto and Bob hadn't moved forward with market research for her area, in spite of her concerns that the tag lines would not play well in Japan or Malaysia. She requested information repeatedly and got back a one-line answer: "We're working on it. Will report back at next meeting."

The other four members seemed to ignore the rift developing in the team. They gave updates at each meeting and had begun coordinating with marketing reps to prepare them for the local launches. They were all smiles to David, but he sensed the smiles were not genuine. He made a mental note to meet one-on-one with the team members. He had been asking for the print ad mock-ups, but the two on the team managing the ads had been evasive, and he'd been too busy to pursue it with them.

After the meeting, David returned to his office to find two messages waiting for him. One was from his boss, asking when she could see the draft presentation for the next week's Executive Committee update. She was anxious to get a briefing on the team's progress and to see the mock-ups for the global ads. The second message was from a team member asking who was supposed to be working on the in-store displays. She thought it was Bob, but he assumed Marcie and her people had it covered. She ended the message asking to whom David had assigned that task.

David rubbed his face and looked at the calendar. One month to go before launch and his superteam was falling apart. He picked up the phone.

If David had called you, what would you have advised him to do?

What Do the Experts Say?

David seems to be forgetting about his role as leader, coach, and communicator. While he is "on top" of what is happening, there is no indication that he is communicating his expectations of performance and accountability to the team. Just because the team has won a game or two doesn't mean that the coach can sit back and let talented players figure out what they are supposed to do.

For me, a key phrase (and opportunity) in the case was, "Although the Bobbseys had missed the deadline for finishing the research, no one said anything and just let them continue to gather data." Clearly, the team has not advanced to a stage where the members could openly address their concerns; however, David could have been a good role model by exploring why the deadline was missed and providing what his expectations were for "catching up." This would have provided clarity for the Bobbseys and for the remainder of the team whose work was being impacted by the unexplained and unexplored delay. To openly discuss the need for meeting the time lines would have not only have helped clarify accountability, but it would have begun to formalize group norms and communicated to everyone that the success of the team depended on mutual support and responsibility. David is getting lots of clues about the developing problems with his team, but seems unwilling to address them directly.

Incidentally, David's boss is providing him with an example of gentle reminders about expectations so she won't be surprised if he is allowing his target dates to slip. Good leaders are seldom surprised by reports at a team meeting because they stay informed through regular "check-ins."

Robert Fulmer
Coauthor, *Growing Your Company's Leaders* and *The Leadership Investment*
Distinguished Visiting Professor of Strategy, Grazidio School of Business and Management, Pepperdine University

There are several issues floating around this case. First, David has not been proactive with his team. He may be assuming that past success will carry him to a continuous high achievement. It's not clear what he has done to ensure that the team maintains a high level of performance. Is it something they could achieve only once? David should get a read on how engaged the team is, whether they find this an important and engaging project. If the answer is no, then he should challenge them and light a fire—he needs to communicate the story better.

A second issue is that the team does not seem to be holding a collective view of what they want to achieve, and thus may not be willing to perceive or support the interdependence that would be required to succeed. Although their deadlines are coming up quickly, it may be worth having the team contract with one another (again), and set some collective goals and accountabilities. What do they need to do and how should they do it? The current model isn't working well.

Marcie may have "checked out" because she does not think she is being heard. She may also believe that she is being denied the resources she needs for success; the Bobbseys have control and, to date, have not taken her concerns to heart. David's perception of their capabilities may be leading him to give them too much responsibility and not enough accountability. David needs to intercede, to understand exactly where they are, why there have been delays in gathering the Asia data, and to show that this project is important.

It also seems MCM is looking for good news in Asia and that might not be a real possibility (another reason to step in with the Bobbseys!).

Michael Serino
Senior Director, Executive Development
Merck & Co., Inc.

Both experts agree that it's clear there are things David should do differently to avoid this situation in the future, but what should he do now? David needs to take swift action.

- There is no time for a lot of one-on-one conversations. Convene the entire team and restate the team goals and top priorities. There is too much splintering and too many people working on their own tasks and agendas. Avoid spending time on blame and how they got to this point. Instead focus the conversation on how to make progress going forward.
- Get accurate updates and status of each task.
- Identify the flexible points:
  - Which tasks are not high priority and can be eliminated if necessary?
  - Which deadlines can change if the need arises?
- Determine next steps, confirm who is accountable for what, and agree to time lines.
- Communicate with and update all external stakeholders:
  - Marketing reps
  - Advertising department
  - David's boss

CHAPTER FIVE

5

HOW WILL YOU WORK ACROSS BOUNDARIES?

IN THIS CHAPTER

The Team in Context ■ Getting Information ■ Providing Air Cover ■ Coordinating with Others ■ Managing Day-to-Day

In Chapter 4, we focused inward, on the role a manager plays within the team, shaping their interactions and culture. But that team doesn't exist or work in isolation. It is part of a larger organization of work and people that can both enable and restrict its capabilities. A team's manager must be active in navigating and managing the work environment that extends beyond the team's boundaries—that is, building the complex networks of systems, people, and resources that are not part of the team.

THE TEAM IN CONTEXT

Teams first need to define and prioritize their goals by aligning with the larger organizational strategy. Next, they will need to get their work done within the context of that organization. Team members will need to define their roles and responsibilities within a larger context, too. Teams operating in an organization are affected by their environment and need to work in conjunction with it—the structure (divisions, departments, hierarchies), policies (education, space, human resources), and systems (information technology, budgeting and procurement, knowledge management).

For example, does the physical layout of the department or division make it easy for team members to collaborate with each other or with other teams? What tools and technologies are available to facilitate the team's work? Do the work processes enable cross-team collaboration and efficiencies? Does the reward system recognize team success as well as individual accomplishments? Can team members get access to the information and resources they need? Is there adequate budget for all team members to receive the training that they need? Is there a process for capturing and sharing knowledge and expertise within the organization?

As the team leader, it largely falls to you to manage the team's connection to the larger environment. This is not to say that you will be the only team member spanning those boundaries, but you will need to consider where connections exist, where they need to be developed, and how best to use them. Note, it's "manage the environment," not manage *within* the environment. Your role is to influence others in the organization, that is, to help shape the policies, systems, and projects that affect your team.

Two social science researchers studied 83 new-product development teams, exploring what communication activities and strategies these teams used to manage their organizational environment. What they found was that the more successful teams—those who met budgets and schedules, and produced more innovative products than the other types of teams—used a comprehensive communication strategy. That strategy involved spending 16 percent of their time communicating with those outside the team. Comprehensive teams reached out to peers as well as top management early on in the project, getting valuable feedback on their designs and establishing relationships that allowed for easier coordination later. They explored options in the environment, but did not get trapped in endless searching. (Ancona, 1992)

It is up to you to help your team to coordinate its work with the outside environment. As we see in Figure 5.1, this may include managing several layers of boundaries and integrating temporary team

FIGURE 5.1 Multiple Layers of Team Boundaries

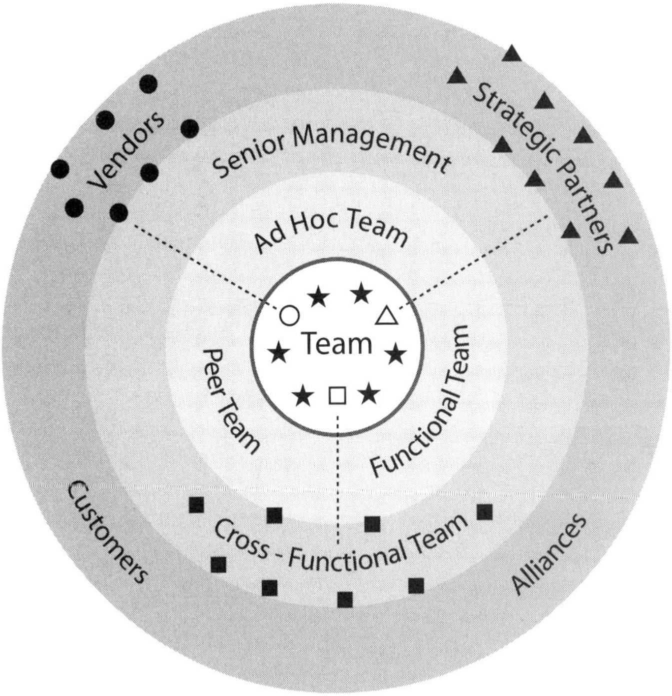

members from various stakeholder groups. Among the tasks are getting information, running interference, coordinating handoffs, and providing critical resources.

GETTING INFORMATION

Some organizations obey a strict hierarchy. Information passes from one level down to the next, or passes laterally across a given level. The manager serves as the main communication channel, relaying any changes in strategy, goals, or policy, and then helping the team make sense of them. In such organizations, a team can become isolated if its manager isn't active in seeking out peers and bosses and doesn't keep track of what is happening in the larger organization.

Even in less strict organizations, managers are critical to information flow. To best help your teams, you need to deliberately seek others out, and make a point of asking for updates. It's almost like a wolf scenting prey on the wind–you need to sniff out any coming changes. Use the beginning and end of meetings for informal chats. Meet someone for a quick lunch. Call and thank someone for good work or for having consistently made life easier for your team. Find ways to keep in touch with peers (and others) across the company.

In addition to getting information, a manager is often the team member who is best placed to *share* information about the team and its work. You are likely to have broader exposure to other departments and stakeholders, and you need to extend this exposure to the work of your team. Just as you may insist that team members attend your meetings, so should you make efforts to attend broader company meetings. You can learn information about other managers' teams, shape how others see your team, and lobby for resources and support for your team. Failing to take advantage of these opportunities can create situations where your team is viewed as less effective or noncritical when in actuality your team is being very productive.

For example, an architectural design firm holds a weekly group meeting of its project managers. Mara, head of a project team working on a museum redesign, has missed the past two meetings. She's also out of the office frequently, and hasn't provided updates on her team's project. Her continued absence makes other project managers suspect she's not working as hard as she should be, when in reality, she and her team have hit a critical point in the project and must devote extra hours to meet a design deadline before the construction crew can begin. Mara's decision not to attend the weekly meetings is hurting her, and she doesn't even know it because she's so focused on the project. If she had taken the time to attend a meeting, her colleagues may have been able to offer advice or resources that could help her team accomplish their project. Plus, others would know how seriously she and her team have taken the project, and could appreciate the extra time she's putting into the museum.

Although it is tempting to only share the good or to stress the important work your team is doing, part of a manager's role is to explore existing or potential problems. You need to raise concerns to upper management, inform them of feedback from your team or your customers, let them know of shifts in the environment, or reset expectations as conditions change. For example, if you were leading a team of EMTs within a small-town fire department, you would be the one to tell the fire chief of the new continuing education requirements your team needs to stay certified. After informing the chief of the facts, you'd have to talk specifically about implications—training funds, days needed, and the like.

PROVIDING AIR COVER

Working in the broader organization requires not only sharing information but also an element of negotiation: when the project is due, who will be working on it, whose turn it is to host the brown bag lunch series, who will take on a new customer. . . . Part of your role is to provide air cover. This means ensuring your team has the right amount and mix of work—saying no to more work when you're already overloaded, and saying yes when it is important or appropriate to do so. This also means allowing them the time and context to experiment with new things.

Consider the case of Ryan, a telecommunications engineer. His company is planning to launch a new communications service in a region of the country they haven't entered before, which is a big deal for the company. The sales and marketing teams are preparing for the launch this spring, with plans to roll out major advertising across television, radio, newspaper, and web outlets. But Ryan has gotten field reports from his team: Hectic winter weather has prevented them from laying fiber optic cable according to the time line. Also, there was a tunnel collapse in one area that got some media coverage—not the best way to enter a new market, but thankfully, no one was seriously injured. Ryan knows the company is counting on the spring launch to boost its profits, but he also knows his team won't be able to reach the deadline without serious help or a time extension. It's up to him, as manager, to take this information to his bosses and renegotiate the deadline or figure out how to engage additional resources.

It can be easier to set clear expectations up front than to have to renegotiate later on. In the example above, future service launches for this company will need to include more lead time for engineering as a buffer.

It may be your decision or you may let the group decide whether to take on new work (or, of course, it may be decided for you). Either way, you need to establish clear expectations with stakeholders: what your team will do and by when, and what they will not do. Agreeing to take on a critical project and deliver results in record time can be a very positive, focused activity for a team. The team pulls together, shares a vision of success, and believes they can deliver together what they could not do alone. On the other hand, taking on many low-priority projects, or projects with unclear deliverables or deadlines, can have the opposite effect. Being clear early on is critical to your success.

Part of being a boundary spanner is understanding when to keep the boundaries solid and when to relax them somewhat. Some managers view themselves as a buffer. They want to protect the team from outside distractions or those who want to infringe on the team's time with noncritical, though time-consuming, requests.

They filter out information–and rumors–that is unlikely to occur and/or that may derail the team's momentum. This is similar to the teacher who tempers a history lesson, revealing the core events and their effects but not the gory details. A manager can similarly protect a team and help them understand what is happening without letting them get mired in detail. Be careful, however, that in your zeal to protect their time and work you don't isolate team members from resources, information, and a larger network of support. Too many boundaries can make them feel disconnected from the rest of the organization.

In your role as manager, you need to understand and manage company politics. This involves building a network within the firm that includes well-positioned people. Well positioned isn't necessarily the same as high ranking, although it can be. What it means is people who are connected to decision makers, experts, and other critical stakeholders. You can be proactive in building a network like this. Call someone to ask for advice; this provides an "excuse" to begin a relationship. Ask someone you know already to introduce you around to others in his or her circle. Volunteer for an ad hoc committee that will give you access to a new set of people.

Another approach is more analytical. Consider the stakeholders who have an interest in the results of your team's work. Map them out and note their relationship to one another and to you. You should think about not just formal (reporting) relationships, but also who has clout, and whose opinion is generally heard and heeded. Next, try to understand the nature of the politics in your organization. For example, is there an "old boys' network" built on longstanding ties? If so, politics may center on the state of those relationships and perceptions of favorites. Is there a group who stepped up to help the company through a hard time and has managed to hold on to their influence even as their strategic importance has waned? Or, is there a group that is currently seen as core to the company, much like the artists at a successful and acclaimed comic book company? They likely have more clout in organizational decisions than the accounting department would, because they are seen as being more tightly coupled to the company's success and harder to replace than others. If you're not in their group, you might figure out how to align with them, to ensure your concerns are heard.

This kind of coordination can be an essential role you play for your team. Smoothing the way for them and buffering them from organizational swings can allow them to focus on their real purpose.

COORDINATING WITH OTHERS

Managers need to consider not only who to align with politically, but also who to align with to get work done. Understand how your team's work connects to what others are doing, and take the lead in building relationships with those groups. Consider which groups provide input to your team, and who receives the output from your team. Which groups should your team coordinate with, and to what degree? Multiple teams and individuals sometimes fall into a trap of working against each other, rather than together. To avoid this, consider who "owns" that relationship–is it your peer leading the other team and you, or is it shared between members of both teams? It is not a one-time event, rather, managing handoffs with other departments is an ongoing responsibility.

Integrating Others

In Chapter 3, we talked about how managers need to support their team with resources and close the gaps if they don't have the current capabilities they need. That discussion focused mainly on how managers build their own teams. Managers can find other ways, however, to supplement their teams without adding head count. They can "build, buy, or borrow" critical resources from outside their teams.

Build. You can and should build a network of people to call on. You may need expertise and advice when a new event or demand comes up. If your need is occasional, it may not make sense to build the expertise in your own team. Rather, you should build network connections to someone else with that special knowledge or skill. For example, if your team is "stuck" on a particular part of the project, one of your peers may have encountered a similar problem on an earlier project and may be willing to speak with your team. If the research your team is reviewing is ambiguous, asking a colleague to review it to provide input may be warranted. Keep in mind that a favor taken is usually a favor owed. You also may be called on to share your team or expertise with someone in your network. (For a richer discussion of how to build your network, see our publication *Influencing and Collaborating for Results.*)

Buy. Where would consultants be if no one bought their (outside) expertise? In some cases, it helps to get an outside opinion or outside input if you need temporary help during a busy time or for a special project. In such instances, it makes sense to rent the resources you need. During tax season, for example, small accounting firms can hire CPAs for a few months. These CPAs work during the busy three month tax season, and then pack up their pencils and leave. Similarly, from time to time, hospitals hire some nurses on a temporary basis. One reason for this may be that they cannot recruit enough permanent staff, so they use temporary staff to bridge the gaps. (BBC News, 2004) Such contract professionals earn more per week than the firm's or hospital's regular staff, but as seasonal or temporary workers, the contractors don't have fringe benefits or the guarantee of stable work. Similarly, a nonprofit organization embarking on a major fundraising campaign may not have the staff resources or board resources to shape the campaign, so they may decide to hire an outside consultant to provide specific recommendations on how to craft it.

You may determine that there are times when it makes sense to buy some extra help, either to tide you through a busy period or as a way to develop your own team. Working side by side with an outside professional can be a great way for your team to update their skills or see other ways of approaching a task.

Borrow. Drawing on that network of yours, you can sometimes borrow people for short spurts to help your team. Some colleges have programs that give a student course credit for working as an (unpaid) intern. If your team's tasks lend themselves to student help, you might be able to borrow a person like this. You get an extra pair of hands and the student gets firsthand experience and exposure to issues not found in textbooks.

Within an organization, some teams are able to lend their members to other departments for fixed time periods. They may have a slack period and the managers there are happy to have their people working, even for another group. For example, framers who have finished framing a Habitat for Humanity home may move on to help the roofing team. Job rotation programs and temporary reassignments are two ways that organizations officially "lend" people from one part of the company to another. These assignments last for a specific period, and although the person coming in becomes a member of the existing team, it is understood to be temporary.

It's your job to decide how your team will meet its obligations: build your internal team, draw on your network, buy outsiders into the team for a specific project, or borrow outsiders to work alongside your team.

MANAGING DAY-TO-DAY

The Situation

Nedra, a project director at BZB, Inc., a software development company, is in charge of revamping one of the company's existing software products. Her team consists of five core members–drawn from marketing, design, and engineering–and several external partners. One of those partners is *Unbreakable,* the company that provides the software security code that BZB uses. Several of the internal development team members are doubtful as to whether the existing security software will still work with BZB's proposed changes, and some of them want to move to another vendor's product with the new release.

Nedra's boss has asked that the project team also include several users from their two primary customer accounts as consultants. Their role is to provide feedback on the usefulness of new features, the look and feel, and how well the new product changes will meet their needs. Nedra met some of the users last year. Their company had installed BZB's software incorrectly, and then went crazy when it wouldn't work. Although a regular software tech could have fixed the problem easily, they insisted vehemently that they needed a senior person. So, off Nedra went, to repair both the system and the relationship. As for the other customer, she has had no contact to date.

Early on, Nedra convinced her boss to allow her internal team members to relocate to a vacant space in the building. Clustered together, this part of the team began to gel. External members would call into meetings via telephone when they could, but rarely came into the office. Contact was rather limited.

Now three months later, Nedra drummed her fingers on her desk, frowning at the phone. The team was progressing well, but a call from her boss had shaken her. The product development budget had been cut, which meant she would have to make cuts of her own. Her boss had suggested both trimming down the features targeted for the revamp and giving up at least one team member. She began working on some scenarios, considering the effect on team morale and the demanding customer user groups. She mentioned the dilemma only to her team leader, Marco. He agreed to begin considering alternatives, too. They didn't mention anything to the rest of the team yet, but would have to soon.

The next day, Marco paid her a visit. He had had lunch the day before with a friend who was working on a product revision team in another division–online photo albums. Although that team had been working on a shoestring budget, their team leader just informed them that their budget had been increased and they would be able to contract some additional help to jump-start their progress. The friend also confided that Mr. Lausier, the director of the Photo Products division, thinks of the revision as his pet project.

Nedra knows that her boss and Mr. Lausier often do not see eye-to-eye on the future direction of the company. She wondered if the other director was responsible for the cuts in her program. Before she could act, though, rumors began swirling about the future of their product and project team. What was just a small budget cutback seemed to now be an indicator of more troublesome trends. Team members grew upset that all the work they had put into the project would be wasted effort, and they were worried about their jobs in general. Nedra could only imagine what the customer user consultants would say once they got wind of the rumors.

What steps would you suggest Nedra take at this point?

What Do the Experts Say?

Nedra needs to have a direct conversation with her boss to understand the environment that gave rise to a cut in her budget. She should ask questions such as:

- Is there a question as to the demand for the product?
- Is the company still committed to the project?
- Is the budget cut a companywide initiative?

- Is this a reprioritization of all budgets, giving rise to cuts in certain programs and additions in others? If so, what were the criteria?
- Are the users satisfied with the product to date?
- Is there an opportunity to revisit the situation?

Assuming the company is still committed to the decision to cut her budget and there is still a demand for her product, a meeting with Mr. Lausier may be in order. At that meeting, Nedra might suggest that one of her team support the online photo album project. This would have the impact of both building goodwill with Mr. Lausier and yet still having access to the team member for part of the time. As a by-product, she would likely get further clarity on his view of her project.

Based on that meeting, Nedra might reconnect with her boss to renegotiate the deliverables. Is it really necessary to reduce features or can the time line be moved? The users can be critical in support of this discussion.

Nedra then needs to meet with her team and be clear on the new goals. Ideally, she can position the discussion in a way that motivates the team. For example, it may be that the online photo album opportunity is an outstanding one for the company and because her team was performing so well, she was asked to give up some of their time to support this new opportunity.

Thomas J. Colligan
Vice Chairman (Retired), PricewaterhouseCoopers

Nedra must act quickly before the situation spirals out of control and further affects her client and the marketplace in which BZB operates. She needs to get the facts and look for creative ways of getting the work done even with the new budget constraint. Her networks and knowledge of the organization outside the team will determine whether she can be successful.

This manager also appears to have not built very communicative relationships with some of her key customers. Although two users from their customer's accounts are external team members, there is no indication in the narrative about Nedra's ongoing relationship with the customers themselves. She went there to fix the problems that emerged but nothing is said about her continuing connection to that customer, and we are told that she has had "no contact to date" with the other customer. She is vulnerable because she doesn't have a relationship or any interpersonal capital to draw on if this current problem gets worse. She is also vulnerable because she is not in touch with the customer about shifting needs, reactions to the current products and services, and so on.

It's probably too late to fix those customer relationships, so Nedra's first step is to schedule a candid conversation with her boss about the origins and meaning of the cut in her program. If she is going to reassure her team, she needs to know the facts about why the cuts occurred, and she also needs insight into whether the doomsayers have any basis for their fears. That conversation will be pivotal to what happens next.

Nedra must know if she has support from her boss. If she does, then she and her boss should have an explicit strategy for helping the team see that the needed support actually exists. If support for the project has waned on the part of her boss, she must utilize her network to see if there are other places in the organization that might provide the support she needs politically. If there are, she then needs to involve her boss to determine if the other source of support is acceptable to him. Can adequate funds be found elsewhere?

If political support is present but funding is not, another option is for her to rethink the composition of her team so that she can complete the project within the tighter budget constraints. Who are the truly core members of this team? What percentage of their time must be committed to this project? Can less critical members of the team be shared with other projects ongoing in the company so that her project doesn't have to carry their full cost? Alternatively, are the skills that she requires to complete her project attainable in another team? Can those assets be shared in a way that contributes to accomplishing the work without busting the budget?

Nedra must pick up the phone and get busy.

Robert H. Reinheimer
Executive Director, Duke Corporate Education, Inc.
Formerly Professor of the Practice of Management, The Fuqua School of Business, Duke University

CHAPTER SIX

6

TAKING THE PULSE AND MANAGING DYNAMICALLY

IN THIS CHAPTER

Staying Aligned with a Purpose ■ Maintaining Team Dynamics ■ Developing the Team's Network

The environment changes constantly–new strategies, work, people, technology, competitors, and stakeholders. Maintaining an effective team is a dynamic process that requires cycling back around to ensure that your work still connects with a purpose, that the team dynamics are enabling the team to work well together, and that the team is developing a network of relationships beyond the immediate team boundaries.

It can be difficult. We have a tendency when busy to focus only on what's in front of us; to be tactical instead of strategic. However, you need to make the time to step back and to see the broader landscape.

STAYING ALIGNED WITH A PURPOSE

You've worked on connecting to strategic goals and objectives in a way that gives purpose and meaning to your team's work and drives their priorities. From your perspective in the center, you are the one who must regularly take the overall strategic direction, consider its implications for daily work, and then translate it for your team. Strategy is no longer a plan that is worked on once a year. You have to continually reconnect your team with the strategy, fill in the blanks, adapt to changes, and readjust your priorities—even while the strategy is changing.

How well do you think the following statements describe your team?

- The company's strategy is clear to us.
- The strategy helps us clarify and define our priorities.
- Our team's objectives are clear and well stated.
- We confer often with other teams across the company with whom we have related projects.

Just as important as your answers is how your team perceives the situation. Do you think your team members would agree with your assessment?

There are a few actions you can take to increase your team's alignment with the broader organization. Use your network to stay connected with what others are working on and talking about, both within and beyond the walls of the organization. Interact regularly with contacts in areas that are most forward looking. For example, the business development, research and development, and new-products divisions are all areas that are watching strategic trends and who are often the first to react.

MAINTAINING TEAM DYNAMICS

How well coordinated and aligned is your team internally? Are you working together and effectively generating results? Coordination, communication, and conflict are three aspects of team interaction that you should keep abreast of.

Coordination

Coordination is critical for teams to be effective. It takes some time for new teams to establish how best to work together, so expect some coordination problems initially on new teams. On established teams, coordination may be taken for granted until problems arise. People often assume that the appropriate individuals were copied on an e-mail, that assignments were clear, or that a critical package arrived on time–only to discover that there were gaps. Other factors can disrupt coordination on a team that has been functioning well up to now, such as team growth, increased complexity of projects, virtual team members, and external stakeholders.

How well do you think the following statements apply to your team? Do you think your team members would agree with your assessment?

- Allocation of tasks is done appropriately.
- Team meetings produce clear "next steps."
- Our team processes and procedures are effective.

Here are some tips for improving coordination.

- Ensure that the team clearly understands its purpose and tasks. Restate objectives and priorities.
- Assess whether the team's resources are being used effectively. Consider shifting some roles and responsibilities to enhance effectiveness.

- Discuss and reinforce team norms: Are people complying with agreed-on standards, especially on communication and decision making?
- Agree on how to record clear next steps as a result of team meetings.
- Make sure that virtual team members are included in all communications, meetings, and events.

Communication

Communication is closely connected to how well you are able to coordinate tasks. Do all team members know what is going on? Some members can feel outside of the communication loop, and there can be many different causes for this. It may be that some members just take longer to trust others, and in time, they will feel more a part of the team. It may be that some cultural differences are operating, making it difficult for some individuals to be clearly understood. It may be that those in close physical proximity forget to update other team members when ad hoc meetings occur.

Some teams develop coalitions, or subgroups, that may be working at odds with the rest of the members of the team. If you notice that communication patterns feel awry or inefficient, think about these and other probable causes. See if as a team you can isolate the cause of an apparent division.

How well do you think the following statements describe your team? Do you think your team members would agree with your assessment?

- Outside stakeholders are kept sufficiently updated on our activities.
- Our team is good at communicating with each other.
- Team members know what is going on.
- We are aware of what each other is working on.

Here are some tips for improving communication.

- Keep people connected through frequent updates.
- Clarify what is important and should have team members' attention. People are often overwhelmed with information from all directions, such as e-mail, voice mail, and written documents.
- Take care to include remote team members in all events and communications.
- Ensure everyone has access to the same information.
- Ensure effective meetings by using pre-agreed-on agendas, alternating times to be sensitive to different time zones, consulting with all members who should have a view, circulating minutes, and allowing reflective breaks for those at a distance to revisit earlier issues. Sometimes there is a great deal occurring in people's minds that is not raised for discussion. Try to understand what's not being said.

Conflict

Conflict is a normal part of team interaction. When focused on tasks and not personalities, it is actually healthy and productive. Avoiding conflict altogether can lead to unresolved issues, frustration, or acquiescence, where everyone agrees and key considerations are overlooked in order to keep peace. Disagreement over tasks can actually help to generate better solutions when people are willing to speak up and voice their ideas—it's called constructive conflict. The team can explore benefits and downsides to different options and brainstorm a wider array of alternatives.

On the other hand, you may be spending more time arguing with each other than working productively on a task. This is not unusual for new teams because members are adjusting to roles where they must give up some control over tasks they used to "own." Within-team rivalries or different preferred approaches or processes also can cause conflict. If destructive conflict persists, however, you will need to take some action to resolve the underlying issues that are getting in the way.

How well do you think the following statements describe your team? Do you think your team members would agree with your assessment?

- We don't argue or have major disagreements.
- We feel free to disagree.
- Team members don't take disagreement personally.
- Team members express their opinions about important issues.

Here are some tips for engaging in the right type and level of conflict within your team.

- If you think some members are occasionally reluctant to disagree, consider a team discussion to explore times where members might have disagreed but did not speak up. Why was this?
- If reluctance to disagree is really a problem, create a rotating role as a devil's advocate.
- Consider whether cultural factors are causing team members not to speak up. Are there members for whom direct expressions of disagreement are not culturally acceptable or considered "rude?" Are members from cultures where disagreement is expressed in nondirect ways? Look for nondirect expressions of disagreement and investigate.
- Help the team understand the need to accept others' rights to different views; demonstrate interest in those views and the value of mutual respect.
- Are there particular triggers or issues that tend to cause conflict repeatedly? Try to address these causes directly.
- Are team members in conflict over project responsibilities? You may consider adopting a rotating "project manager" style of organizing tasks. For a particular objective, one person is given the authority to divide up tasks, assign roles, allocate resources, and make final decisions. The others will have similar opportunities in the future.

DEVELOPING THE TEAM'S NETWORK

The last piece of the puzzle is staying aligned to the world beyond the core team. You need to take the lead in developing and maintaining relationships for your team. Make connections and stay in touch with the people who make key decisions or are well positioned for access to information, news, and advice. Keep your team's needs aligned with the resources and expertise available in the broader organization.

As a boundary spanner, you need to set expectations with others and understand their expectations. Then, adjust your team and its outputs to work with those external dynamics and changes. You broker the deals for people, deliverables, resources, status, access, and anything else the team needs from or needs to give to another group or stakeholder.

How well do you think the following statements describe your team? Do you think your team members would agree with your assessment?

- We have access to all the expertise we need.
- When we need help from other areas of the company, people are generally available to help.
- Outside stakeholders are kept sufficiently updated on our activities.

Here are some tips for improving alignment with stakeholders.

- Don't let connections end when the project does. Stay in touch with the people you have made connections with–and keep these relationships fresh.

- Protect and nurture the team's credibility with that network of external relationships. If new information or challenges come up, call to let them know right away.
- Continue to explore the challenges you have in common.
- Help your external contacts make connections with each other, because they are seeking to strengthen their networks as well.

CHAPTER SEVEN

7

GROWING TRENDS

IN THIS CHAPTER

Technology Makes Global Teams Possible ■ Global Teams Face Complex Issues ■ Making It Easier

In this book we have discussed the fundamental role that a manager plays in leading a team–keeping the team aligned with a purpose, ensuring it has the right mix of members and capabilities, and managing the dynamics within the team and with the outside environment. We have discussed three factors that make managing the fundamentals more complex: speed, distance, and blurring boundaries. As Figure 7.1 reflects, these challenges and forces are all interconnected and moving swiftly.

We've also alluded to some of the changes we are seeing in the ways that organizations are using teams. We'd like to explore the trends we're observing in the business world a bit more, and offer some thoughts on how to deal with them going forward. These trends will increase the complexity of making the gears run smoothly for your team. You already may be experiencing them on a daily basis, or they still may be emerging within your organization.

FIGURE 7.1 Team Gears at Work

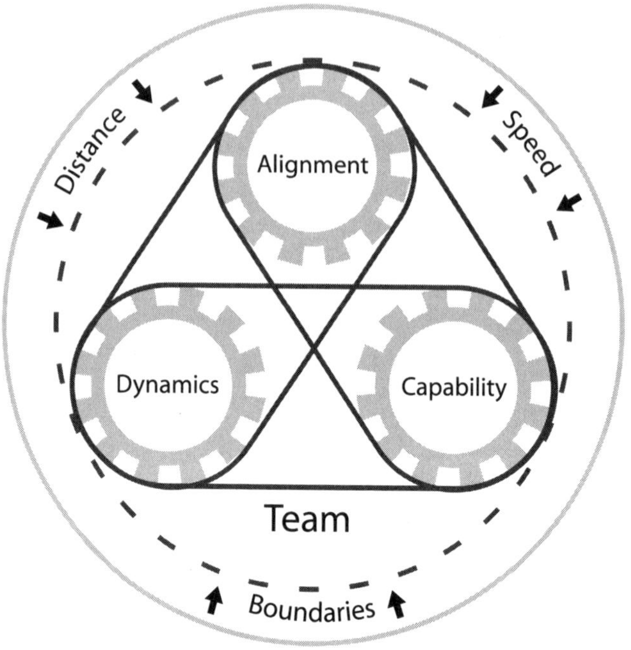

TECHNOLOGY MAKES GLOBAL TEAMS POSSIBLE

The number of virtual teams continues to increase. Technology improvements have reshaped the way we think about distance. In the 1970s, making a long-distance telephone call was pricey and seen as a special event–"Don't talk more than a few minutes; it's long distance!" Now, the price for long distance in the United States is minimal, or nonexistent. International calling is also commonplace and inexpensive. Not only can we connect with someone who is on another continent, but we can talk to several people on several continents at the same time; conference calls routinely link people in disparate locations.

In addition to talking easily with those far away, we can see them. Plane travel is more prevalent, and video conferencing is becoming more reliable as a replacement for travel. The world is shrinking, and it is easier (and cheaper) than it ever has been to connect to people around the world.

As a result, more businesses have spread their operations and customer base over a broader geographic area. A research and development (R&D) department might have multiple labs in India, England, and the United States. A parts supplier might set up production alongside a key customer's assembly plants in Mexico, Spain, the United States, and Thailand. The supplier then can run each location as a separate subsidiary or try to coordinate across the sites. If top management decides to coordinate across the sites, they will likely call in one or more teams of managers in the center of the organization and ask them to manage the integration and alignment issues. These teams are virtual teams by necessity. Layered on top of that, they are cross-functional as well.

In addition to setting up shop close to customers, some organizations are setting up shop where labor costs are lower than in the headquartered country. "Smart sourcing" takes jobs and moves them to other locations. However, the responsibility for managing the people who have those jobs may not move. Suddenly, a manager finds his or her team is in three countries instead of down the hall. That manager may find that the team's role has been outsourced to another company and he or she needs to manage the relationship with the vendor's employees.

Some companies have ad hoc needs and they assemble a representative group to meet them. For example, a company that has 12 sales groups spread around the globe may want to have an internal conference to share best practices. So, the VP of global sales assembles a conference-planning team from 4 continents that will need to decide the content, speakers, venue, logistics, and the like. As another example, the Human Resources department for a Global 1000 company may want to develop a new format for performance appraisals, so the home office team recruits delegates from 15 offices around the world to comment on and beta test the new format. By getting input, they hope to smooth the way to a successful rollout and to create criteria that are culture neutral.

GLOBAL TEAMS FACE COMPLEX ISSUES

Although companies want the anticipated benefits that come from close coordination between functions or locations, they have yet to adjust their internal structure, systems, or culture to support them. Take a large food company as an example. It wants to align its snack foods divisions around large geographic areas. It assembles a team made of two R&D managers (one for baked goods, one for confectionery), three manufacturing managers (one from each of three plants), a sales manager, a purchasing manager, and three marketing managers (each with responsibility for different products/brands). The company expects these ten peers to work collectively to increase market share and presence in this widespread geographic region. It expects them to align to the overall company's goals and bring their various functional groups along.

Unfortunately for this team, they will have a hard time coordinating their efforts, given the problems associated with the way the larger organization is set up.

- *Identity issues.* Members of this team identify with their home function. Their business cards have functional titles, not cross-functional titles, and their professional development is in their function. Their loyalty isn't to this new team.
- *Reward or recognition issues.* Team members continue to have their functional boss conducting their performance appraisals and deciding their pay/bonus levels. Their "other job" carries more weight.
- *Resource issues.* If the cross-functional team needs any resources, whose requisition codes do they use for the request? Who sponsors their efforts?
- *Alignment and strategy definition issues.* Each member of the team has a set of goals that aligns to a functional or divisional strategy. The cross-functional team as a whole, though, does not have clear goals or strategy.
- *Influence issues.* Peer teams have to rely on indirect influence and obligation to outside stakeholders, as no one has authority over the other members.

- *Authority issues.* The larger organization works within silos based on functional structure. Members of the cross-functional team can't speak for their silos and definitively commit their home departments to anything. The members may agree to a course of action but then each one has to go back and sell it.
- *Cultural issues.* This team has people from six nations, four professional backgrounds, five different native languages, and four different locations. The mix of customs and subcultures means the team doesn't have a set of shared norms, language, or work processes. Just coordinating among them will take effort.
- *Coordination issues.* The team is spread across four time zones and two work shifts. They don't see each other and may not all make it on the same call. Decisions sometimes stretch across two or more meetings.

Some of these examples may seem extreme; but these patterns are becoming more common and are not unique to a single industry. Together, they are increasing the complexity of the manager's challenge of getting the team to deliver the desired results. If you were a manager on this team, what would you do?

MAKING IT EASIER

If you are a manager who finds himself or herself on a team like this—virtual, cross-functional, or both—how can you make it work more effectively? For a long-term or ongoing commitment, you need to invest in the fundamentals of working well together. As we noted in Chapter 1, in that respect, virtual teams are like other teams, only more so. All the steps outlined in earlier chapters still hold, only the accountability shifts from you as the team's manager to shared accountability among all the members on the team. The virtual team of peers needs:

- A clear purpose
- The appropriate members and resources to fulfill its purpose

- Effective operating routines
- Members who manage the team's boundaries and relationships with outside stakeholders
- To take stock periodically and make adjustments

In addition, you need to find ways to address the special circumstances these teams find themselves in. These teams are usually ad hoc or begin as ad hoc teams that then get institutionalized, that is, the broader organization finds the team valuable and keeps it operating semipermanently. Given that these teams are ad hoc, the solutions to the problems they face should also be ad hoc. You should look to manage the issues as they arise, plan for the ones you can anticipate, and keep flexibility for the team.

If you were to take that advice, what would it look like? *First, you would consider what to request when the team is first put together.* What are known problems that you can try to avoid? As mentioned earlier, communication is critical. Therefore, having an information technology communication infrastructure to support your team is an essential element.

Dual identity and no clear authority back in the functions is another problem. When the team is set up, figure out how to *get the authority that you will need.* Establish expectations and decision-making routines with the function's stakeholders at the start. Be clear how you will work with them, and that you will have the function's proxy in the cross-functional team meetings.

Continuing the authority theme, be sure you (the team) *have a senior-level sponsor* who can help make things happen and who can bridge different networks within the larger organization. For example, this team should have a budget. Who can make that happen for you and your peers? If a member has trouble implementing back in the function, who can he or she call for help?

Given the nature of the project, the members should be recognized and evaluated on it. So, when setting expectations, be clear with your manager that this project or team assignment is significant and should (on an ad hoc basis) be considered in your performance review.

A final item to address up front is *getting the virtual team together face-to-face early on,* and on occasion later. Although most of the work will be done long distance, the team needs to "break bread" together and establish some personal connections. (Here's one place that budget comes in handy.)

Once you have managed the outsiders and gotten those key elements lined up, *what can you do as a team to bridge your distances and differences?* First, integrate quickly. As a team, you need to build strong relationships among yourselves. To do that efficiently, you need "face time" where everyone can meet together. Spend that time on building norms and your relationships. The tasks can wait for more regular meetings.

Next, set a norm to communicate early and often. When teams aren't in the same place it becomes easy to drift apart and lose touch with one another. Make it a point to keep in regular contact.

Communicate openly. Everyone is in the same situation, having split obligations between this team and their functional group. As you make decisions, discuss constraints openly. Find ways to support one another as you each go back and try to sell the decision. Even with the support you lined up earlier, you may still have authority wrangles. Once committed to any action, though, your word is your bond–if you can't do something, say so, or else you must follow through on promises. No one has time to chase other members; each has to self-manage.

Finally, the other part of your job is to *be the catalyst for broader change.* Identify the main issues and try to quantify the consequences or impact of misaligned reward systems, work processes, people capabilities, and resources. Practice communicating the issues and the opportunities to your boss and your boss's boss in a way that demonstrates an understanding and commitment to fixing things. A critical part of your job as leader of a team is to shape the conversation and raise the issues in a way that shows you have thought about things systemically, identified the opportunity, and are clearly part of the solution, not the problem.

If you and your team manage well, ultimately the systems in the organization will change to better match the work. You, though, only need to work on ad hoc solutions to your local problems. The rest will follow in due course.

BIBLIOGRAPHY

Ancona, Deborah, and David Caldwell. 1992. "Bridging the Boundary: External Activity and Performance in Organizational Teams." *Administrative Science Quarterly* 37: 634–665.

Anonymous. 1996. "Whoa, Team!" *Journal of Business Strategy* Jan/Feb 17(1): 8.

BBC News, UK edition. 2004. "Costs of Temporary Nurses 'Soars.'" (Monday, 1 November).

Belbin, Meredith R. 1993. *Team Roles at Work.* Massachusetts: Butterworth-Heinemann.

Brooks, Frederick P. 1975. *The Mythical Man-Month.* Philippines: Addison-Wesley Publishing Company, Inc.

Dumaine, Brian. 1994. "The Trouble with Teams." *Fortune Magazine* (September 5): 86–92.

Fenn, Donna. 1995. "Teams: Second-Stage Snags," *Inc. Magazine* (November).

Hackman, J. Richard. 2002. *Leading Teams: Setting the Stage for Great Performances.* Boston, MA: Harvard Business School Publishing Corporation.

Janis, Irving. 1971. "Groupthink." *Psychology Today* (November): 43–46, 74–76.

Job, Ann. 2004. "All Female Team Designs New Volvo." *The Detroit News,* 3 March 2004.

Kelley, Tom, with Jonathan Littman. 2001. *The Art of Innovation.* New York: Doubleday.

Katzenbach, Jon R., and Douglas K Smith. 1993. "The Discipline of Teams." *Harvard Business Review* (March-April).

Krzyzewski, Mike, with Donald T. Phillips. 2001. *Leading with the Heart: Coach K's Successful Strategies for Basketball, Business, and Life.* New York: Warner Business Books.

LaFasto, Frank, and Carl Larson. 2001. *When Teams Work Best.* California: Sage Publications, Inc.

Lewis, Clive. 2004. "Being Creative in the Workplace." *British Journal of Administrative Management,* (October/November) 43: 24.

McCaskey, Michael B. 1996. "Framework for Analyzing Work Groups." Harvard Business School, 1 August 1979, Revised 22 November 1996.

Rayner, Steven R. 1996. *Team Traps: Survival Stories and Lessons from Team Disasters, Near-Misses, Mishaps, and Other Near-Death Experiences.* New York: John Wiley & Sons, Inc.

Russell, Bill. 1979. *Second Wind: The Memoirs of an Opinionated Man.* New York: Random House.

Thompson, Leigh L. 2004. *Making the Team: A Guide for Managers.* New Jersey: Pearson Education, Inc.

Walsh, Susan, ed. 2004. "Woodrow Wilson Bridge Replacement: Progress over the Potomac," *PB Bulletin,* 20 (3) (April).

Weiss, W.H. 2002. "Building and Managing Teams." *Supervision.* 63 (11) (November): 19–21.

Yamashita, Keith, and Sandra Spataro. 2004. *Unstuck: A Tool for Yourself, Your Team, and Your World.* New York: Penguin Group (USA), Inc.

Index

A

Accountability, 4, 45
Action Learning Associates, 42
Ad hoc teams, 4, 19, 81, 84
Air cover, 61–63
Alignment, 2, 8
  checklist, 23
  global/virtual team issues with, 82
  of goals/organizational strategy, 57, 72
  with purpose, 71–72
Allocation of tasks, 73
Aspirations, personal, 31–32
Authority issues, global/virtual teams and, 83, 84
Ayers, Dick, 33

B

Baseball expansion teams, 37–38
Belbin, Meredith, 42
Body language, 5
Boston Celtics, 30
Boundaries, 2, 3, 11, 57–70
  coordinating with others, 63–65
  information and, 59–61
  managing day-to-day, 66–70
  multiple layers of, 59
  providing air cover, 61–63
  purpose clarification, 19–20
  team in context of, 57–59
  working across, 57–70
Brooks's Law, 36
Budgets, 38, 58

C

Capabilities, 2, 3, 7, 8–9
  aspirations/goals and, 31–32
  borrowing or buying, 36, 64–65
  building, 25–32, 64
  checklist, 39
  closing gaps in, 35–39
  comfort with assigned tasks/responsibilities, 30–31
  consultants and, 36–37, 64–65
  defining, for effectiveness, 28
  determining, 29
  five-step gap analysis, 29
  mix of team members and, 26–27
  skills inventory, 29
  team chemistry and, 29–30
Challenges, 2–3, 5
Change, manager as catalyst for, 60, 85
Chemistry, of team, 29–30
Coaching, 31, 35
Coalitions, 74
Collaboration, 6, 8
Colligan, Thomas J., 68
Commitment, 4, 14, 22, 82
Communication
  comprehensive strategy of, 58
  connectedness, 49–52
  consistent, 44, 50
  core messages, 50
  of existing/potential problems, 60–61
  global teams and, 84, 85
  improvement tips, 75
  managers and, 59–60
  in meetings, 75
  obtaining information, 59–61
  team dynamics and, 74–75
  virtual *vs.* co-located teams, 5
Community, 5, 38
Complementary skills, 3

Complexity, 3, 82–83
Conference calls, 80
Conflict, 20, 49, 75–76
Constructive conflict, 75
Consultants, 36–37, 64–65
Context, of projects, 7, 8, 16, 57–59
Coordination, 14, 73–74
Coordination issues, global/virtual teams and, 83
Costs, 38
Credibility, 78
Cross-functional teams, 4, 6
Cross-team collaboration, 58
Culture, 3, 5, 74, 76, 83

D

Devil's advocate, 76
Distance complications, 3, 11, 85
 purpose clarification, 19–20
 virtual teams and, 5–6
District of Columbia Department of Public Works, 18
Diversity, of team, 38
Duke University, 26
Dynamics, 2, 9, 71–78
 alignment with purpose, 71–72
 communication and, 74–75
 conflict and, 75–76
 coordination and, 73–74
 facilitating of efforts and, 7
 maintaining, 73–76
 within team, 41–42
 team network, developing, 77–78

E–F

Expectations, 4, 43–45, 77
 communication and, 44
 measuring, 45
 renegotiating, 61–62
Federal Highway Administration, 18
"Fist, The," 26
Focus, 38
 multiple points of, 42–43
Friction, 6
Fuhrman, Russ, 18–19
Fulmer, Robert, 55
Functions, team organization by, 42–43

G

Gaps, 29, 35–39
Global teams
 complex issues and, 82–83
 coordination problems, 82–83
 management and, 83–85
 needs of, 83–85
 trends, 80–82
Goals
 alignment with company strategy, 15
 clarity of, 8
 commitment to, 22
 personal, 31–32
 planning and, 9
 priorities and, 21–22, 57
 purpose and, 22–23
 shared, 3, 18
 SMART, 22–23
 team capabilities and, 28
Groupthink, 43
Growth opportunities, individual, 31

H–I

Hyde Tools, 33
Identity, of global/virtual teams, 82, 84
Influence issues, global/virtual teams and, 82
Influencing and Collaborating for Results, 50
Information
 resources, 32–34, 58
 sharing, 60, 75
Information technology
 communication infrastructure, 84
 support, 34
Integration, 85
Interactions, 52
Interactivity, 4
Interdependency, 4

J–K

Janis, Irving, 43
Job rotations, 65
Jones, Bobby, 31
Krzyzewski, Mike, 26

M

McHale, Kevin, 31
Management teams, 4
Manager(s)
- as buffers, 62
- as catalyst for change, 85
- communication and, 49–52
- company politics and, 62, 63
- connecting to larger environment, 58
- day-to-day management, 52–56, 66–70
- of global/virtual teams, 83–85
- group norms and, 46–49, 74
- multiple points of focus of, 42–43
- outside presentations by, 9–10
- priorities and, 38–39
- role in effective team-building, 2–3, 7–10
- senior-level sponsors, 84
- setting expectations, 43–45
- team capabilities, assessing, 9
- team network development, 77–78

Maryland State Highway Association, 18
Meetings, 14–15, 73, 74, 75
Mentoring, 31
Milestones, negotiating, 39
Misdirection warning signs, 14

N

National Basketball Association, 30–31
Negotiating, 39
Networks, 64, 77–78
New product development teams, 58
Nonverbal communication, 5
Norms, 46–49, 74
- defined, 46
- explicit, 48
- individual concerns/preferences and, 49
- subtle/unstated, 46–48

O–P

Olsson, Hans-Olov, 27
Opportunities, personal, 31
Outcomes, 22–23. *See also* Results
Parsons Brinckerhoff, 18
Performance reviews, 84
Personalities, team organization by, 42
Perspectives, 34
Physical work environment, 58
Planning, 9
Politics, 62, 63
Potomac Crossing Consultants, 18
Priorities, 21–22
Project manager, 76
Projects, ensuring context/meaning of, 7, 16
Project teams, 4
Purpose
- across distance/boundaries, 19–21
- alignment of, 8, 71–72
- clarity of, 13–14, 21–22
- global teams and, 83
- goals and outcomes, 22–23
- shared, 3, 4, 18
- strategy and, 15–19

R

Reinheimer, Robert H., 70
Relationships, managing, 2
Resources, 2, 7, 8–9
- closing gaps in, 35–39, 64–65
- effective use of, 73
- information access and, 32–34
- issues with global/virtual teams, 34, 82
- supplying, 32–35

Results, 13–23
- alignment checklist, 23
- purpose across distance/boundaries, 19–21
- strategy and, 15–19

Reward/recognition, 45, 58, 82

Rivalries, 75
Roles, team organization by, 42
Ruddell, Jim, 19
Rummel Klepper & Kahl, 18
Russell, Bill, 30

S

Serino, Michael, 56
6th Man of the Year Award, 30–31
Size, of team, 38
Skills inventory, 29
SMART goals, 22–23
Smart sourcing, 81
Speed, 2, 3, 10
Stakeholders, 63, 74, 77–78
Strategy, 72
  alignment of team goals/ company strategy, 8, 15–19
  building purpose with, 15–19
  definition issues, 82
Subgroups, 74
Success
  analysis of past, 34
  clarity of purpose, 13–14

T

Team(s)
  boundaries, 2, 3, 11
  chemistry, 29–30
  common pitfalls of, 43
  complications of distance with, 3, 11
  considerations when building, 38
  defined, 3–7
  dynamics of, 9, 42–43, 71–78
  factors affecting, 2, 3
  global, 80–83
  guidelines, 3–4
  manager's role in building effective, 2–3, 7–10
  network, developing, 77–78
  speed and, 2, 3, 10
  strategy and, 72
  temporary members of, 36, 65
  types of, 4–5
  value of, 1–3
  virtual, 5–6, 80
  warning signs of misdirection, 14–15
Technology, 1
  complications of distance and, 11
  global/virtual teams and, 5, 80–82
  team resources and, 32
  telecommunications, 5, 80
Telephone calls, 80
Temporary team members, 36, 65
Training, 31, 35–36, 58
Trends, 79–85
Trust, 51, 74

U–V

URS Corporation, 18
Value, 2
Video conferencing, 80–81
Vincent, Fay, 37
Virginia Department of Transportation, 18
Virtual teams, 5–6
  see also Global teams
  coordination of, 74, 82–83
  purpose and, 19–20
Vision, 8
Volvo Cars, 27

W–Y

Walton, Bill, 31
Woodrow Wilson Bridge Replacement, 18
Work environment, 58
Your Concept Car project team, 27–28